The Raw Food Feast
7 Days Through the Rainbow

by Mandilyn Canistelle

ISBN: 978-0-9816954-3-3
Printed in the United States of America
First printing.

Published by
Growing Healthy Homes LLC
P.O. Box 3154
Bartlesville, OK 74006

To obtain additional copies of this book, please visit
www.GrowingHealthyHomes.com.

Text and Recipes by Mandilyn Canistelle
Food styling by Peter Cervoni
Cover design by Hannah Hopkins, Aim High Photography
Photography by Hannah Hopkins, except for photos on pages 65 and 77 by Sera Johnson
Book design by Sera Johnson
Editing by Laura Hopkins

Chef Mandy's assistant: Marke McConnell
Prep chefs: Trisha Heddlesten, Pepper Ann Hernandez and Laura Massenat
Kitchen assistants: Pamala van der Veldt and Cathy Thomas
Chef Mandy's Stylist: Tonya McLing

Required disclaimer: The information given in this book is for educational purposes only and is not intended as diagnosis, treatment or prescription for any disease. This is a compilation of the author's beliefs based on independent research and professional and personal experiences. The reader is advised to seek the advice of his or her chosen health professional before adhering to any health regimen. The author and publisher bear no responsibility for the use or misuse of any of this information. The decision to use or not to use any of this information is the sole responsibility of the reader.

If you have a health-related question or a health challenge, please seek the guidance of the health professional of your choice. Growing Healthy Homes LLC is not able to answer health questions.

Dedication

To Brad, as we begin the next chapter in our lives. May our life together be an example of God's love, provision and restoration.

To my eight children Kinley, Hayley, Kaden, Hunter, Holly, Roma, Keziah and Khloe. May you be rooted in God's Word and enjoy His perfect health.

Acknowledgements

The journey that has culminated in the production of this book would not have been possible without the support and love from so many people.

Thank you to my parents, Bob and Katha Bardel and Ray and Elaine Hansen, for your continued love and support in all of my adventures.

Thank you to the love of my life, best friend and husband, Brad O'Neal, for your patience and understanding in all my raw endeavors and aspirations. You have helped me in all areas of my life.

Thank you to my twin sister, Mindi, and restauranteur brother, Wayne. You have invigorated me with tips and advise that have influenced my crawl, walk, run and flight.

Thank you to my children for sacrificing so much by allowing me the time to complete this book, for sampling all the recipes and giving me thumbs up or thumbs down.

Thank you to Bea and Ken Sprouse for encouraging me to begin this health journey and helping me pursue my dreams with your endless love and care of my children.

Thank you to Impact Productions for your convictions and love for our world and how you have shaped my destiny in so many ways, such as in this published work.

Thank you to Peter Cervoni, my professional mentor. You have been generous with your expertise and boundless knowledge of food and have encouraged me to press forward. I can never thank you enough for graciously agreeing to be the food stylist for this book.

Thank you to Tim and Diane Dillingham for introducing me to Young Living Essential Oils, which has inspired this raw recipe book. I am grateful for your friendship.

Thank you to Karen Hopkins for being my educator and model for essential oils. Your motivation and revelation helped to bring this book to reality.

Thank you Growing Healthy Homes LLC for the countless hours and dedication to bring this project to fruition and your faith and confidence for God's purpose in my life.

Many thanks to Marke McConnell, Trisha Heddlesten, Laura Massenat, Pepper Ann Hernandez, Cathy Thomas, Pamala van der Veldt and Tonya McLing for your instrumental role in this project. Your hours of dedication, gifts, talents and creativity is appreciated and admired. You gave unselfishly and filled every position and more!

Thank you, especially to my Lord and Savior, Jesus Christ. I am grateful for the tests and trails that have strengthened and encouraged me. You have been my provider through the storms of life and have given me an array of experiences as colorful as the rainbow.

Table of Contents

Introduction

The Feast of Nature

Foods grown on the vine, on the tree or in the soil primarily are used in raw food cuisine and consist of uncooked, organic, enzyme- and nutrient-rich fruits, vegetables, leafy greens, nuts, seeds and sprouts. Raw foods are whole foods that God has provided through nature in their freshly harvested state. Living foods are raw foods that have been sprouted, germinated, cultured and/or fermented to increase their nutritional value. Living foods abound in nutrition because of their increased enzymes and the pre-digested condition of their nutrients, which make them easier for the body to assimilate and eliminate.

Unlike manipulated and over-processed foods, raw and living foods — provided by a loving God through His Creation — nourish the body and return the love and joy of eating without the guilt that is associated with gluttonous consumption. Many people approach the subject of food seeking solutions for improving health, increasing energy and resolving weight issues. Most have a misconception that a healthy diet must necessarily limit great-tasting foods. We are designed by our Creator to enjoy all the flavors and textures of food in its natural state; this includes salty, spicy, savory, sweet, bitter and pungent. Flavors and textures are for our enjoyment as we refuel our bodies.

Nourishing the body does not have to be complicated. The toil of weighing ingredients, counting calories, logging daily intake and calculating fat grams is not necessary when consuming good, natural foods. This is because the culinary art of raw and living cuisine encourages food production from high-quality ingredients that preserve life rather than harm it. It is possible to prepare an unlimited number of recipes, including family favorites and traditional dishes, without using heat or animal products. Consider the various properties of the foods found in nature. They are easy to obtain, tasty, appealing to children and adults, organic and free of toxins, edible in their unprocessed state, easy to digest, a meal unto themselves and full of healthy calories and micronutrients to produce fuel for the body.

All life-threatening disease does not stem from eating poorly, but eating healthfully can be preventive and healing. Education and research helped me stick to my new convictions about diet. Below is a collage of topics that gave me the information and inspiration to press forward while understanding the issues that were pertinent to this lifestyle.

Vitamins, Phytonutrients and Minerals

Most vitamins and phytonutrients are destroyed or damaged when heated above 105°F. Heat also changes the composition of some organic minerals, diminishing bioavailability — or the absorption in the gut. The difference between fresh and cooked food is starkly contrasted: a bowl of raw vegetables is more vibrant in color than a bowl of cooked vegetables. The cooked version loses its color through the process of oxidation when food is heated.

Enzymes In Food

Enzymes are necessary for every function in the body and are the most heat-sensitive of all nutrients. If they are destroyed, these vehicles cannot distribute vitamins, phytonutrients and minerals throughout the body. Raw fruits, vegetables, nuts and seeds have built-in enzymes necessary to digest them. When fruits ripen, they are digesting themselves by changing their starches into simple sugars; this is why unripe fruit is not as sweet. Enzymes were intelligently designed in nature to aid our digestion of food designed in nature.

Enzymes In The Body

When enzymes in food are damaged by heat and commercial manufacturing, the body must use its own enzymes to digest the damaged food. This is problematic on two counts. First, the body has other uses for its own enzymes such as rebuilding and repairing cells. Second, the body must now perform two tasks using the resources that were previously only performing one task. When the body does not have time to complete its work of digestion and cellular repair, junk food is stored and dead cells remain. This causes rancidity in the body that reveals itself through a decrease in energy, sickness and disease.

Five years ago, I gave my children a tangible example of the effect a lack of enzymes in junk food has. We purchased a fast food burger with fries to calculate how long it would take before it decomposed. To this day, it has not changed in appearance, except to shrink a bit and petrify.

Water

Our bodies are 70 percent water. We need to consume clean, pure water to sustain life. There are many companies that offer high quality drinking water; I recommend alkaline/ionized water from a reputable company. Common advice is that we should all drink water upon rising, as well as, between meals. For the raw foodist this remains important. However, because raw fruits and vegetables are rich in naturally filtered water, raw foodists are consuming a water-rich diet and have a lessened need for extra water.

Proteins in Natural and Unnatural States

Vegetables and fruits naturally provide a percentage of their calories from protein. Nuts, seeds, high-protein greens and sprouts, algae and green powders can meet the slightly higher protein demand of pregnant women, athletes and others.

A high-protein animal diet is the primary source for unnatural proteins. People have achieved weight loss by consuming a high-protein animal diet, however, this is a dangerous way to attain desired weight loss results. In these cases, weight loss is achieved through a process called ketosis. In this process, ketone — a strong acid that is harmful to our bodies — accumulates when the digestive system uses fat instead of carbohydrates for energy. These animal proteins usually are prepared by heating the protein to high temperatures; the heat damages the proteins, causing the amino acid chains to congeal. These large protein molecules may be unusable and even harmful to the body, causing inflammation and other problems.

Fats in Natural and Unnatural States

Unheated fats are utilized by the body and contain antioxidant properties. Heating fats causes them to lose their antioxidant qualities and become carcinogenic. Heating fats also makes them sticky, which can cause blockages in the arteries and digestive tracts, inhibit the absorption of nutrients, and reduce the body's ability to transport oxygen.

Imagine the perfect God-created avocado or nut packed with good fats and then picture a greasy casserole dish or skillet. It usually requires scouring to remove the residue that is caused from leftover fatty foods. I do not believe we have any cleaning agent as harsh as a scouring pad in our arteries to remove these heated fats that clog our systems.

Is it any wonder millions of people in America suffer from heart attacks each year?

Digestion
The type of food and how it is grown greatly affects good digestion. The simple carbohydrates in fruits and vegetables are readily available as fuel for the body. It is best to eat tree- and vine-ripened produce, rather than produce that has been picked early to have a longer shelf life. Some companies store their produce as long as six months to a year. If a fruit or vegetable doesn't taste vibrant, it could be unripe and grown in soil without proper minerals. Avoid eating produce from inorganic companies.

A good example of this is the ripening process of the banana. Ethylene is a gas naturally emitted by many fruits, and it causes fruits to ripen quickly. Bananas naturally emit low quantities of ethylene, but are highly sensitive to it. Clearly even the most conscience produce companies cannot avoid this natural ripening process as ethylene can accumulate when produce is stored and transported. However, some companies harvest produce early to get the most shelf life from it and use ethylene gas to ripen it. A banana that develops the natural speckled brown spots as it ripens, has not been overexposed. However, if a bright, perfect yellow banana does not pass through the brown-speckled stage, it has been overexposed to the gas and will not have the wonderful flavor of a plant-ripened banana. In all my years of providing organic produce, the organic banana, is one that I consider to have a significant taste difference than that of the conventional banana.

Assimilation
Assimilation requires energy and the proper catalyst — those show-starting enzymes — to help distribute the food to particular areas in the body. Raw, natural foods have high quantities of vitamins, phytonutrients and minerals along with a native supply of enzymes that make them available to the body.

Elimination
Good digestion aids in good assimilation and, finally, good elimination. All three are essential to good health. The soft, soluble fiber in fruits and tender, green vegetables makes them easy to digest and assimilate and aids elimination. Elimination ends the process either well or poorly depending on the health of the body. It is necessary for the body to flush toxins out of the body rather than storing them.

The Body in an Acidic State
Processed food, pollution, stress and cooked food diets — consisting of meat, dairy, sugar, starches, grains and caffeine — leave most people's pH balance too acidic. This prevents optimal cellular activity and immune system function. An unhealthy, acidic pH state leaches alkaline minerals from the body.

The Body in an Alkaline State
Organic produce is alkalizing. It cleanses, heals and maintains a body's natural functions, encouraging a healthy and active lifestyle. An alkaline state is good for all the parts of the being: mind, body and soul. It is difficult to concentrate, exercise, meditate or worship when the body is plugged up with acid-forming junk. When choices are made to keep the body pure, everything works freely with focus, energy and spiritual awareness.

Raw Food and Essential Oils

Raw food sustains and maintains, while therapeutic-grade essential oils recognize invaders, flush them from the body and restore balance. When food and essential oils work together, it is a powerful union.

Essential oils are the aromatic, volatile liquids distilled from plants — obtained from the seeds, roots, flowers, leaves and bark. Each plant may contain hundreds of molecular chemical compounds. The majority of plant essential oils are obtained by steam distillation to release the plants' precious oil.

There is one company —Young Living Essential Oils (YL) — that I trust. YL's proprietary steam-distillation process uses low heat, proper pressure, precise timing and fresh, properly grown and harvested plants. Therefore, it is very important to use only high-quality therapeutic-grade essential oils right from the farm. YL has more than 4,500 acres of aromatic farmland.

Cheap, synthetic oils are potentially toxic. Any product that is labeled 'for external use only' is not safe for external or internal use. Skin is the body's largest organ. Why can the largest organ be exposed, but not internal organs? That is illogical. Anything that I put on my skin or breathe should be able to be ingested as well. If I can't eat it, it doesn't belong in, around or on my body.

Using YL oils in food preparation is beneficial and supportive of the entire body, but especially the digestive, immune and adrenal systems. Because excessive heat also can change the chemical composition of essential oils, they complement raw food well.

Only a small amount of essential oil is needed in food preparation because the oil is very potent and powerful. Unlike dried herbs and even some fresh herbs, which have started to decompose, the oil is the life-blood of the plant and is living after proper distillation. Essential oils, unlike fatty oils, have a never-ending shelf life. Viable, potent oils have been discovered in ancient tombs.

The Raw Know-How

Now that you are versed in the basic benefits of raw food, you need to know how to take action. The techniques in this book are designed to be efficient, easy to learn and remember, and provide great satisfaction. This book provides a variety of techniques with patterns throughout the day that make food preparation fun.

My goal is to entice everyone — especially the very susceptible career-oriented, busy parent and the single young adult — to consume quality foods without always eating out. Many raw living restaurants have opened throughout the world. They are nice to visit on occasion, but cost and convenience is still not as easy to attain as having healthy alternatives in the home. Because raw cuisine is a new concept, most everything must be prepared from scratch. In time, companies will begin manufacturing raw staples and sauces to simplify preparation. Meanwhile, we can enjoy the time in the kitchen to learn about the many varieties of produce and ways to create dishes without destroying the life of the food.

The Raw Food Feast is a seven-day plan of tried and true recipes with step-by-step instructions, beginning with the colors of the rainbow and ending in a rainbow of juice feasting. Each day represents ingredients that are the designated color for that day, spotlighting a fruit, vegetable, nut or seed that will be used throughout the day's production. It is very satisfying to realize that a rainbow of raw foods has been eaten and enjoyed throughout the week.

Some people have the time to prepare elaborate gourmet cuisine, while others need fast solutions to eating healthier. It is important to be equipped either way in order to make lasting changes and accomplish this goal on a regular basis. There must be a strategy put into place. New equipment and techniques are applied. New storage and kitchen organization needs to be set in place. Being prepared is helpful in a raw kitchen in order to continue on the path of healthful and beneficial patterns. Below are tips to guide even a culinary novice through kitchen organization.

It can be frustrating and overwhelming if you are not prepared, so I have included all of the information you will need, including grocery lists. If you cannot purchase everything at once, begin with the recipes that you can make and add them to your daily routine.

This plan is a beginning. Have fun and expand into other ingredients using the same idea and patterns that this book provides. As you equip yourself, you can move forward in this journey with confidence and purpose.

Raw Equipment

Knives
With all the tools available to the modern kitchen, a knife still is the most important tool. With so many brands, sizes and styles on the market, choosing a knife can be a daunting task for a home chef. A collection of knives in every shape and size is not necessary. Most jobs in the kitchen can be covered by just two: a chef's knife and a pairing knife. I prefer the lightweight Japanese kinds, but European styles are acceptable.

Juicer Extractors
Because of the many types and brands of juicers on the market, it is important to select the one that best fits the application for which it will be used. The three types are centrifugal (spins to extract), masticating (grinds to extract) and gears (crushes to extract). The centrifugal types are the least expensive and have the least ability to juice variety. They juice fruit well, but do not juice greens. These are used in most commercial settings. The masticating type is a well-rounded juicer and good for most all applications. It produces foam, which is undesirable, but can easily be removed before drinking. The gear types are great for juicing greens, but not good with fruit or vegetable fruits. They are the best for keeping the juice's integrity by not warming the juice as it is extracted.

The Raw Food Feast uses a variety of produce, both fruit and vegetables. Therefore, it is recommended to use the masticating type for the recipes in this book. I prefer owning both a Champion (the masticating type) and a Super Angel (the crushing twin gear type). I juice my greens through the Super Angel and utilize my Champion for fruit and other vegetable juices.

Electric Citrus Juicers
It is advantageous to choose a citrus juicer that continues to rotate after lifting the fruit off of the rotating extractor in order to press the juice from the leftover pulp with a spoon and scoop the pulp out without stopping the machine. I prefer the Warning Pro, since this juicer is the sturdiest and longest lasting of its kind. I do not recommend the citrus juicers that stop after lifting the fruit off of the rotating unit.

High-Speed Blenders
Choose a sturdy, high-speed blender that specializes in blending almost anything. These machines liquefy, cream, grind and even juice. If a smooth juice is desired using a blender, the ingredients will need to include a liquid, for example filtered water, to assist with blending. Then the mixture will need to be filtered through a juice bag to remove the pulp. The Vita-Mix brand is my choice for a high-speed blender. The manual knobs allow me to control the blending process and

apply techniques in order to reach the consistency that is desired.

Food Processors

In raw cuisine, there are a variety of desired textures that are best accomplished with a food processor. A blender cannot replace the techniques required by the food processor. The width of the container and the speed of the machine play a large role in reaching the desired consistency for pates and crusts. Most raw recipes serve six to eight, so choose a food processor with the largest container. For home use, I prefer the Cuisinart brand, which offers a large container.

Food Dehydrators

Choose a square design with a fan on the back to ensure adequate space and even- drying. These machines are used in a variety of ways. They reduce vegetables and fruits for soups, sauces and pates. They dry breads, crackers, wraps, roll-ups and other snacks. This machine is equivalent to the oven in traditional cooking, yet allows drying at lower temperatures to preserve the integrity of the food. The Excalibur brand is my choice for the many applications that are required for making creative raw cuisine.

Raw Techniques

Many of the techniques used when preparing raw cuisine are no different from preparing food before cooking it. If you purchase the equipment above to begin your raw food feast, be sure to follow the manufacturer's instructions and become familiar with the operating and safety information. This will allow you to be comfortable and confident as you begin this plan.

I use the spatula technique often. This is the process of gently separating the mixture from the corners of the high-speed blender to help create a vortex — the tornado effect that forms in the middle of the mixture while blending — without using the cumbersome tamper, which is difficult and messy to control. Of course, leaving the lid open while blending with a spatula can provide some hilarious and explosive moments. When the method is mastered it is the preferred technique for assisting the blending process for thick and creamy textures. The action of the vortex is important for the mixture to combine, but can be hampered when bubbles form under the blade. This is one reason why the Vita-Mix brand is preferred; it allows for a dense mixture without needing to add additional water to blend.

Each day **The Raw Food Feast** begins with a reduction recipe. In standard culinary terms, a reduction is a liquid mixture that has been simmered to reduce its volume and the process makes it thicker and intensifies its flavor. A raw reduction is simply dehydrated, maintaining the nutrients of the food, while reducing the liquid to intensify the flavor. This process helps to lesson the need to add more spices and additional ingredients to season the dish, which increases the cost of the recipe.

Because there is no waste in a raw kitchen, I designate a scrap bowl to store any leftovers from other food preparation. At the end of each day in **The Raw Food Feast**, there is a recipe that utilizes the ingredients from the scrap bowl. This is a technique that is satisfying for the taste buds and the wallet.

Raw Preparation System

The acronym P.R.E.P. is used in each recipe to help organize raw food preparation in stations where each step is completed. Misé en Place, the French phrase meaning "everything in place," should be practiced in order to set up and review recipes for necessary ingredients and equipment. Being organized with a system, including the correct setup of adequate equipment and tools, will encourage a peaceful and enjoyable atmosphere so your love will be the most important ingredient included during each session in the kitchen. These stations and steps defined below will assist the creation of the meal and Misé en Place.

Prep – The station where any work noted in the ingredient list is completed, such as soaking, cutting, chopping, etc. Also, this is the stage where all ingredients are gathered. In addition, a cutting board, discard bowl, knives, hand towels, apron, hair cover, gloves (if preferred), sink and other tools of choice should be clean and in place for the preparation of the produce listed in the ingredient section of the recipe.

Run – The station where the ingredients run through the particular machines to naturally process the food to desired textures. Detailed instructions are provided here.

Ease – The station where the name says it all. This is where a component to the recipe or the recipe itself rests in the dehydrator, in the freezer, or in the refrigerator until it is ready for use. Also, this is the time to make things easy by properly labeling and storing ingredients for later use.

Present – The station where the artist in you shines. Before enjoying these delectable dishes, use these instructions to add the final touches. Garnish instructions are included to help the creative process and are optional for plating. Have fun!

Raw Ingredients

The ingredients chosen for this book should be available year round. If an ingredient is difficult to find organic, then choose conventional (nonorganic) or make a substitution. However, it is important to make an effort to purchase all organic and fresh, unless frozen organic is specified. Let it encourage those to journey on the path towards the end of the rainbow where health and healing await. Enjoy the journey!

Filtered water is a primary ingredient in many recipes. Distilled, ionized, spring or other clean, pure sources of water are common drinking water choices for many. Refer to the Raw Resources on page 143 for preferred water systems.

References to Young Living Essential Oils are listed as YL. Refer to ordering information on page 145.

Raw Storage

It is best to freeze or refrigerate nuts and dehydrated items. They may be stored in airtight containers in the pantry and may last three to six months. However, each item should be monitored regularly for freshness.

Milks and coconut water should be used within two or three days after they are made, while cheese can be used up to seven days.

Re-sealable freezer bags are best for freezing items, while glass containers with lids are preferred for refrigeration. Air sealers, such as Food Savor units, are recommended to assist with shelf life; storage of this kind still needs refrigeration and should not be mistaken for traditional canning by heat methods that allow for pantry storage. Recipe components and leftovers can be refrigerated longer when the air has been removed. It is best to label all items prior to storing.

Transition to Raw

Food has many associations other than nutrition. Emotional and seasonal patterns are very strong and should be considered when making changes. When offering this food to those you love, gently encourage them to try the new recipes by introducing the raw cuisine as a prequel to their other favorite cooked dishes. I do not suggest replacing everything at once, nor expect your loved ones to be on the same page as you are. Be patient with your family and friends. It is important to introduce this concept with grace and consider your own journey that led you on the road to raw and living cuisine. Otherwise, you may discourage your loved ones from trying these flavorful combinations and miss a wonderful opportunity to teach and lead by example.

The goal of a transition is for your family to learn to feast on raw food with excitement and grateful attitudes without the feeling of forfeiting their favorite meals. **The Raw Food Feast** is a great place to start in that it includes my raw versions of many of my family's favorite dishes like pizza and pasta. Another good starting point is a routine I use to this day. We begin a meal eating something raw — and eating all of it — before eating something cooked. This usually is a choice of raw fruit or soup before lunch and a big green salad or raw dinner entrée before dinner. Typically, they are full immediately upon eating the raw offering and do not eat as much of the cooked item. Clearly, the cooked item is the hook to get them to try raw, but the routine reinforces that nutrition is found through raw food not cooked.

The following are suggestions for serving cooked entrees with the raw dinner entrees. These work well with my family and still are easy for me without too much more time spent in the kitchen.

Day 1 - Yellow Squash Tomato Pasta with a health-food store bought organic pizza

Day 2 - Nori Red Pepper Hand Rolls with steamed rice and organic stir-fry vegetables

Day 3 - Carrot Dill Romaine Wraps with baked potatoes (sweet, gold or red)

Day 4 - Sunflower of the Sea Lemon Pate with a seasonal cooked vegetable platter

Day 5 - Eggplant Truffle Fettuccine with bruschetta topped with fresh tomatoes

Day 6 - 'Roasted' Tomato Broccoli Pizza with whole grain pasta

Prepare to Detox

When one begins a period of fasting, toxins that have built up in the body from years of gluttonous behavior begin to be released. This process can temporarily overwhelm the body and cause sickness, aches, fever and all manner of discomfort. It is good for the body to be ridding itself of these pollutants, but it can be very discouraging for the person experiencing it. Most people misinterpret the detox process and blame their negative symptoms on an outside germ, on the diet change itself or even on the cleansing products used. Too often these people halt their fasts prematurely and return to their SAD (Standard American Diet) state of eating, rather than pressing ahead through the detox symptoms and into better health.

Exiting a fast too quickly unnecessarily taxes the resting digestive system before it has time to restart. During these times of detox the body begins to operate in a greater state of cleanliness. By returning immediately to solid food, old and familiar cravings can be stirred and lead to bingeing. It is better to slowly reintroduce the various flavors and spices back into the diet. A good rule of thumb is that for every day of water fasting, allow half a day of juice feasting before reintroducing blended foods. Following this, fruits and other easily digested foods can be consumed without objection and, finally, wholesome solid foods. The goal is to never return to the SAD way of eating, but rather to choose foods that heal and nourish.

The first steps that I took into a raw food lifestyle were juice feasting and water fasting. I wanted to quickly rid my body of years of junk food distress. Even so, it took me a solid 12 months of cleansing my system with fasts, juices and wholesome raw foods to feel truly detoxified. At times during my detox year, it seemed that I was sicker than I had ever been in my entire life. To make matters worse, many close friends and family were not supportive of my changes. They had misconceptions and concerns for my well-being, but I had thoroughly researched the process and knew the telling signs of a detox. Because I knew all of this beforehand, I was not afraid of my own detox symptoms when they showed up and actually welcomed the periods of toxin release. However, I did not treat fasting lightly. I gradually entered a fast by reducing solids in my diet and then gradually exited by slowly re-introducing solid foods to my diet.

Start Feasting
The Raw Food Feast provides a week's worth of food with daily production plans. However, feel free to alter the plan to fit your lifestyle or the number of servings. These recipes are designed to yield six servings, but less can be made. Be mindful that because this is a multiple-day plan with all of the scraps being used, halving a recipe might have an impact on other recipes. Cross-references are provided for all recipes that yield leftovers to be used in other recipes. For example on Day 1, the scraps from spiralizing squash are used in the dehydration bread recipe at the end

of the day. You may prefer to spread out the days to allow more time for preparation until you become more comfortable and proficient in the kitchen with this new style.

There is much attention to detail and the tips are precise so you can be efficient in the kitchen. Patterns are repeated to help save time. For example, morning production always starts with reductions in the dehydrator that will be split between the meals to be prepared and flavored in unique ways. Breakfast always starts with a fresh extracted juice. Lunch always is a blended soup with a cracker or bread from the previous evening's dehydration. The afternoon snack is a smoothie that is used to make candy roll ups in the dehydrator. Dinner spotlights the vegetable of the day, which coincides with the color chosen from the rainbow. Dessert is either a parfait for that evening with enough to spare to make into a pie for the following day. The evening production ends with dehydration from the extra ingredients leftover from the day of raw food production. These techniques and patterns and the use of the same fruit, vegetable, nut or seed throughout the day in different ways helps make the preparation more simple.

May you be blessed and encouraged as you begin this journey. Move forward with the understanding of why this food was created for you, how your body uses it and the confidence that you can make new, healthy, substantial habits that last.

Start feasting!

I have fond memories of my childhood years, growing up with a creative mother and an adventurous father. My entrepreneurial parents instilled in me a passion for contributing to society in a positive way that brought enjoyment to people's lives. My father was the proprietor of a Mexican restaurant in north Oklahoma City, and my mother owned a dance studio, which provided wonderful opportunities to entertain the community throughout the year. For my twin sister, Mindy, and me, dancing became our passion and primary focus.

As a dancer, the days leading up to a performance were filled with treats. A candy fiasco proceeded the big night with a pizza party ending the evening to reward our achievements. I remember the celebration and the time it took to recoup from the festivities more than I do the actual performance we were celebrating. I felt horrible from all the junk. Many recitals were accompanied by a week of sickness that followed.

On the contrary, when I was sick and should have been flooding my system with fresh juice and water, I succumbed to cravings in order to soothe the pain. My favorite sick meal was grilled cheese with tomato soup plus a concoction of 7-Up mixed with concentrated orange juice. It seems silly to me now, but even as an adult I was lured to fix this comfort meal during the colder months or when I felt melancholy.

Although I didn't realize it back then, my emotional patterns connected to unhealthy comfort foods and

Left Picture:
Mandy with children (clockwise)
Kaden, Roma, Khloe, Keziah, Kinley

created long-term problems for me. This was setting destructive patterns for me, as food always accompanied my emotions — the highs and the lows. As a teenager, I used to pride myself in not succumbing to the peer pressure of using drugs and alcohol. However, I spent years indulging, splurging and bingeing on junk completely unaware of the dangerous pitfalls of these habits.

"I succumbed to cravings in order to soothe the pain."

When I was fifteen, tragedy struck my fairy-tale world when my parents divorced. This emotional storm came during a time when divorce was not yet the common occurrence it is today. Almost instantaneously, I had new stepparents and a whole new life. My perfect concept of family — safe and secure in small town America — was shattered.

During our senior year in high school, while still recouping from all the change that had transpired in our home, Mindy and I auditioned for and joined a touring dance company, Impact Productions. We graduated from high school on the road and had the time of our lives alongside other equally enthusiastic teens and young adults on an amazing adventure that took us to every state in America. The director of the company and his family were devoted and zealous Christian role models. With biblical application, they motivated us daily before we performed on stage. I am forever grateful for those two years of growth. I later came to think of this as an intense, integrity-filled, two-year schooling, which would inspire and define my life. I would grow out of my childish ways into an adulthood that was permeated with hope.

When it was time to leave, I advanced with a spiritual strength in Christ that would give me the confidence to face any circumstance, no matter the duress or delight. I was optimistic that my heavenly relationship would always supply me with the ability to overcome, achieve and imagine dreams to come true.

Through these early adult years, my battle to balance diet and exercise raged. My strict workout regimen did not harmonize with my lousy food selection. I operated a dance studio and retail dance store and sustained myself through the day with coffee and Diet Pepsi. Each morning I ran four miles to work to teach dance. At the end of each day, I ran four miles back home and crashed on my sofa. For dinner, I would devour air-popped popcorn dipped in picante sauce alongside my habitual bowl of fat-free frozen yogurt. I fancied my low calorie, low fat diet. Then, one day I awoke to a wrenching ache in my abdomen. After resisting the pain for most of the day, I finally was convinced something was critically wrong. My mother rushed me to the doctor, who rushed me into surgery for an emergency appendectomy to remove my ruptured appendix. After the operation, the doctor revealed he had found an imbedded profusion of popcorn kernels in my appendix. Never in all his years of appendectomies had he seen such a case.

After my recovery, I became reacquainted with Todd, my junior high boyfriend. We began attending church together and became engaged. My fervor for managing a dance school quickly morphed into energy for organizing a wedding and then a home. During our first year of marriage, we learned we were going to be parents. For me, the joy of approaching motherhood and of governing a household replaced the career path of dance. For a time, life was a bed of roses, and I was in denial that roses do have thorns.

I delighted in following in my mother's footsteps of studying cookbooks, developing recipes and creating food. However, idolizing both fitness and food left me feeling conflicted and ultimately unhealthy. My exercise regime did not counter my excessive desire to eat all kinds of foods, particularly during my first pregnancy. I figured since I was bound to lose my figure anyway, I might as well savor every morsel of food I had avoided as a dancer. Every night I indulged in anchovy, pepperoni and triple cheese pizza, with ice cream for dessert. I withdrew from exercise — that positive drive had completely dissolved — as back pains, swelling ankles and heartburn filled my days. Despite these physical troubles, I continued to feed my unborn child and myself whatever suited my fancy. When it came time to give birth I opted for an induced delivery instead of natural labor, due to gestational diabetes that arose temporarily during late-term pregnancy.

"I was in denial that roses do have thorns."

My firstborn daughter, Kinley, was subjected to this free-for-all food frenzy, provoking health challenges for her, as well. Oblivious to the cause, I prolonged my indulgent conduct, not realizing that the basis of her pain came from indirectly ingesting the junk food, particularly dairy and starches, which with I comforted myself. Kinley awoke daily with matted eyes and interrupted every nursing session with projectile vomiting. She was relentlessly colicky and congested. The pediatrician diagnosed her matted eyes as under-developed tear ducts. I was told to simply tolerate the condition until her tear ducts had time to fully develop over the course of a year. As for the projectile vomiting, the doctor proposed formula as a supplement to avoid dehydration, never once associating the mucus discharge as my daughter's reaction to dairy ingested from the mother's milk she was drinking. Her body was rejecting the vices that I embraced nightly. Years later, the connection of matting eyes with dairy was confirmed when my third child was subjected to one of my dairy sprees and likewise awoke with matted eyes. But when I refrained from dairy the onslaught of ailments ceased.

I wanted to make good food choices, but I had limited knowledge. I tried to follow the recommendation from the medical community and government to consume five fruits and vegetables each day and to eat foods of a variety of different colors. As I tried unsuccessfully to follow this advice, I was overwhelmed and eventually surmised that it was a lofty and unattainable goal to consistently consume this quantity of fruits and vegetables. I would do well for a time but quickly run out of ideas to keep things fresh and varied.

My lackadaisical choices inadvertently caused further fluctuations and imbalances in my family's health. I resolved to remain steadfast as a full-time mom and housewife, enjoying every minute. Still, the conflict between feeling energized, healthy, active and thin battled with my love for preparing and fabricating all kinds of not-so-good-for-me foods. There seemed to be a constant and varied stream of afflictions, from constipation to chronic illness. Worry, anxiety and confusion consumed my days as I obsessed over these health maladies.

The infuriating part was that no one seemed to take these prevalent conditions seriously or validate my concerns when I attempted to seek answers. The hours I should have spent enjoying life were instead squandered at the doctor's office, in bed or nursing a

child back to health. I wrestled with the mainstream practices of administering routine shots, allocating prescription antibiotics for sickness and positioning tubes in ears to prevent earaches.

I soon realized that my entire reaction to infection and disease was motivated by fear. At the first sign of any sickness, I promptly scheduled appointments with the doctor's office, aching for that magical prescription which would make everything better. I placed doctors on a pedestal and depended on their aptitude, all the while ignoring their advice to change my diet to include five fruits and vegetables daily. I did not take responsibility for my own actions and instead continued to tolerate the consequences that afflicted both my family and me. This became a never-ending battle that I accepted as a way of life.

It wasn't until I felt extreme pains in my lower back and abdomen that I began to seek other answers. I was diagnosed with Irritable Bowel Syndrome (IBS), which could potentially lead to colon cancer. I had just given birth to our son, Kaden, and could not fathom suffering from what I surmised was an elderly person's disease. I was dumbfounded when I had difficulty getting pregnant a third time and then when that pregnancy ended in miscarriage. The pain in my stomach did not cease and was affecting all areas of my life. Eventually, I called upon God. After praying, the answers came immediately, but it took months before I was ready to listen.

My mother, with whom I'd always had a very close-knit relationship, had expressed her earnest desire to share some audiotapes with me on the subject of diet and health. Believing it was some sort of marketing gimmick for a new weight loss miracle drug, I wasn't interested. Mother would not reveal much, only that I would be intrigued to discover these simple ideas about health that would be beneficial for me and my family to adopt. It was another month before I decided to actually listen to the dreaded tapes. To my great surprise, they contained basic facts, presented in layman's terms that were simple enough for anyone to put into practice. It was all about how our bodies are designed to function on natural sustenance provided by God from nature, free from antibiotics, over-the-counter drugs and medicines. I wholeheartedly adopted this scientific, medical information and began to learn to feed my body proper foods so it would run smoothly. I learned the body's red flag was sickness, and it was there to alert me that all was not as it should be.

The results of that profound moment undid all my years of searching for the best way to eat for balance. My reason for dieting switched from the vain motivation of losing weight to an emphasis on sustaining health. I suddenly had a growing passion to prepare a variety of foods from nature. The options, I discovered, were varied and many in each new season of the year. It was gratifying to observe my old appetite for fast food transform into new cravings for wholesome fruits and vegetables. I knew this new outlook of a natural lifestyle and diet would finally sustain me and give me hope for a healthy, energetic life, free from sickness and disease.

But I quickly learned that just because I excitedly shared my new lifestyle with the people around me, it did not mean they were going to feel motivated to follow suit. In fact, my blabbing to everyone who crossed my path—whether they wanted to hear it or not—just caused unnecessary grief for me and awkwardness for them. Unless I was intimately involved in a particular person's life, I learned to share my discoveries only with those

acquaintances who asked me about them, rather than the other way around. This point was driven home frightfully for me as I forcefully volunteered my newfound food wisdom to an acquaintance who was doing her best to elude the conversation while our children played at the park. The following week, as friends and family celebrated my two-year-old daughter's birthday, a knock at the front door interrupted our party. Two women announced themselves as caseworkers with the Department of Human Services (DHS). I was confused and shocked, but remained calm. The ensuing interrogation encompassed the exact topics I had discussed at the picnic with my acquaintance.

As commanded, I gathered my little ones, who had just filled their large platters with beans, rice, salsa, tortillas and vegan enchiladas. Of course, I encouraged them to bring their fiesta fare to meet the ladies on the front porch. The women visibly relaxed with their first glimpse as my children ate and enthusiastically answered their questions. Before long, we were all engaged in a healthy food conversation. The caseworkers divulged that the report that had been filed against me had accused me of causing my children to suffer from malnutrition. Based on the alleged descriptions in their report, the two women had expected to come to my house and find three very sick, emaciated children. What they found, instead, was quite the opposite and before departing, they both requested my business card with the intention to learn more about this way of eating.

Despite the case against me being dismissed, the two women apologized for the unnecessary need to still follow through with the DHS guidelines. I would be required to give an accounting of the growth and health of my daughters for a period of time following the unexpected visit. I was told a pediatrician would monitor my girls on a weekly basis for the proceeding six months to ensure their adequate maturity. My healthy-but-petite children weighed in below "normal" on the American charts, which caused the doctors concern at the beginning, however, after all the appointments were complete, each of my daughters received praise for steady growth and consistent health.

It was a scary wake up call to realize the impact my family's lifestyle changes could have, even on strangers. But the difficulties didn't only stem from outside sources. Throughout the early years of changing my family's diet, I also endured misunderstanding, persecution and disdain from extended family and friends. But I could not imagine returning to the miserable state of sickness that I had previously lived in and set as an example to my family. Unlike previous years, I now welcomed the future. I had found the truth and the truth had set me free—free from my lifetime of struggle with food.

This God-given consciousness would nourish me through unexpected difficulties that lay ahead on my path of life. Fourteen years and five children later, I would have a new challenge to walk through; I found the thorns in the rose bed of my marriage. Unaware that the life I loved was about to come to an end, I was faced with divorce and my dream of happily-ever-after fading away.

The divorce of my parents was hard enough to endure as a young teen, but as a homemaker and mother of five with no formal college education and a heart for my family, living through it myself was paralyzing. I was advised to begin exploring my career options so I could share in the financial responsibilities of the divided family. I elected to work toward an occupation that would satisfy my

inclination to focus on health, specifically in natural food preparation. In the seven years since my desperate prayer, I arrived at a fresh, innovative way of preparing foods through the art of raw cuisine. It was a bittersweet moment in my life but as I was about to discover things were about to get a lot more colorful!

Many in the raw food world follow a path that is influenced by New Age thought and practice, which holds a positive view of alternative health treatments, self-guided healing and disease prevention through healthful lifestyle practices. While I do not align myself with the spiritual and religious ideas that are espoused by many New Age followers, I do value their approach to preemptively seeking health. At this stage in my life I found that my personal universe needed a fresh change. I needed to seek health again—physical health, emotional health and health in my relationships with my children. These are the reasons why I eat and prepare raw food.

My journey into raw food began in October 2004, in Harbon Hot Springs, California, at the Living Light Academy. Many months of conversation and discussion with the director, Cheri Soria, preceded my decision to enroll. She was very accommodating and patient as I figured out a way to attend this world-renown school. Arrangements were made for my children to be cared for while I traveled to the West coast for a month of intense schooling in raw and living cuisine preparation.

Knowing the mountainous landscape in California would present a greater physical challenge than the level plains I was familiar with back home, I came prepared to hike, walk, jog and exercise in my surroundings each day before classes started. I quickly learned where to pick fresh, delectable figs for breakfast alongside the stream I crossed on the way to my classes. I loved to breathe in the beauty of God's country while simultaneously side-stepping the many shrines hidden there, dedicated to all kinds of contrasting gods.

At Living Light, school days, instruction and homework infused every moment. My fellow students and I received training in the FUNdamentals, Essentials, Chef/Instructor Training Series, and Elegant Entertaining and Catering, so that we could be prepared for a career as educators and professional chefs after our studies were completed. I esteemed my season there and enjoyed meeting new friends. The expert staff was delightful, accommodating and exceptional in every way. (I was among the last group of students to experience the peaceful hippie resort in Harbon Hot Springs. Soon thereafter, the institute relocated to the Mendocino Coast, in the small town of Fort Bragg. It since has grown and developed into the most successful raw culinary school in the world.)

Prior to graduation, we were instructed to pen a life motto. I drew my inspiration on the final stretch of a three-mile run back up the steep mountain towards Harbon. I meditated through tears of release, thankful to God for His presence and protection. As I lifted my eyes, an isolated tree on the highest peak far ahead gleamed in the morning sunrise. It seemed to stand courageous and somehow thrived on that steep mountaintop. "If that tree could survive," I thought to myself, "surely God could keep me purposed with His never-ending streams of living water and I could be fruitful to help others and myself." A favorite Bible passage from Psalm 1:3 then came to mind and I personalized it as my motto. "I am a tree planted by streams of water, which yields its fruit in season, whose leaf does not wither, but whatever I do will prosper."

I returned home from Living Light recharged and invigorated in time for a Thanksgiving reunion with my children. There were many options available to me for bringing the idea of raw cuisine to my local community. I pledged the remaining months of the year to recipe development and to constructing my plan of action. I established a small school from my home the first year and expanded the programs offered with each consecutive year that followed. In addition to teaching, I catered elegant meals, wrote and demonstrated raw recipes and encouraged community outreach through raw potlucks.

Other opportunities presented themselves to glean further education from raw food experts around the country. I learned additional culinary skills necessary to face the challenges that would unfold along this natural career path. Soon, I was hired by a company that organized health-promoting vacations throughout the world. I counted myself privileged to hone my kitchen and catering skills while traveling with them to numerous exotic locations.

"... surely God could keep me purposed with His streams of living water..."

I also reconnected with my old friends from Impact Productions, the dance troupe with whom I had traveled while in high school. The director's wife was fighting a life-threatening disease at the time, but had chosen to treat it holistically rather than turn to conventional drugs or surgery. I had the honor of sharing my food knowledge with her. She and her husband then hired me to host a regular segment on a television health program they were producing for natural health expert Jordan Rubin. This experience allowed me to polish my television presentation skills and become more adept at demonstrating my raw food dishes to an audience. Through these channels, I eventually attracted the attention of people influential enough to help me realize my dream of founding an educational center for raw and living cuisine that housed not only a restaurant, but a store and a culinary school, as well. I co-developed this modern, state-of-the-art, raw facility — 105degrees — in my hometown.

To commemorate the advancement of my raw food career, I sought a new last name, my professional moniker. On the way back from one of my culinary excursions with my good friend and talented chef, Peter, I stopped at a famous South Florida fruit stand called Robert is Here. There was an abundance of exotic tropical fruits for sale at this stand, most of which were foreign to me.

One particular fruit had a brilliant yellow outside with creamy, buttery meat. As I was savoring each bite, Pete noted that the name of the fruit I was eating would make a beautiful girl's name: Canistel. I took to it immediately and pronounced it to be my new working name. We changed the spelling to Canistelle to represent a more feminine take on the name. I combined my middle name with my first and made it official at the courthouse. Mandy Lynn Catania became Mandilyn Canistelle, with aspirations that one day Canistelle would become my middle name when I remarried.

The inspiration gained from interacting with incredible chefs and educators, transitioning my own children to raw food and teaching other kids has been the driving force for my book for children. My personal experience tells me that kids are generally willing to try anything as long as their own hands prepare it. They enjoy the challenge and are intrigued with the large quantity of unique, available produce. In the book, I plan to incorporate the use of therapeutic-grade essential oils and raw food, to promote natural healing. I desire

to teach the next generation the truth about the purest foods (those that are raw and living) and medicines (essential oils) that can undo the consequences of indulging in the fast food lifestyle. It will incorporate seasonal produce and introduce children to a world of new and unique foods provided by God through nature.

My goal of demonstrating the powerful combination of natural foods and essential oils holds true for this book. My desire for the readers of **The Raw Food Feast: 7 Days Through the Rainbow** is to inspire all to join me in this raw food journey and take a stand against the processed junk food that is so tempting and so readily available to us and our children. I want to rally a growing movement of conscious eaters who live by the ideal that little by little we can make a difference.

We need to stop thinking that changes in food choices would cause too much upheaval in the family, cost too much or take too much time. To the contrary, chronic illness from sticking with the old food choices causes too much upheaval in the family, costs too much and takes too much time. The sooner you and I speak with our choices, the sooner the market will come to make those choices as available as the junk food is now.

So, while I am a chef and neither a medical doctor nor a nutritionist, I can attest that food has been used as a healer in my own life, just as it has been a conduit of health in the lives of many others, from many cultures and over many centuries. I have found that a healthy food regimen eliminates poor choices, which helps with time management, and provides nourishment and health that allow me to focus and balance the other areas of my life. **Freedom never tasted so good!**

Base Recipes

Frozen Bananas

Prepare prior to Day 1 for use on all days.
Yields 29 frozen bananas

Bananas, 29

1 Prep
Peel bananas and divide into halves.

2 Ease
Freeze the bananas in labeled, re-sealable bags for smoothie and candy recipes on Days 1 to 6. Prepare 5 bananas for Day 1, 4 bananas for Day 2, 4 bananas for Day 3, 4 bananas for Day 4, 5 bananas for Day 5, 7 bananas for Day 6.

Soaked Dehydrated Nuts

Prepare for use Days 4, 5 and 6.
Yields 4 cups soaked dehydrated pecans, 2 cups soaked dehydrated almonds and 1 cup soaked dehydrated walnuts

Note: Nuts are easier to digest after they have been soaked. The practice of soaking is encouraged in order to remove the nut's natural protectors, releasing the enzymes to allow access to the nutrients. Drying returns them to their crunchy state, and they are ready to be used in recipes requiring dry nuts. Pecans, almonds and walnuts double in size when soaked. They reduce back to original size when dehydrated. This recipe refers to the dry quantity.

In three separate bowls:
Raw pecans, 4 cups (14 ounces), soaked 4 to 6 hours
Raw almonds, 2 cups (10 ounces), soaked 4 to 6 hours
Raw walnuts, 1 cup (4 ounces), soaked 4 to 6 hours

1 Prep
Drain and rinse the nuts. Place on three separate mesh dehydrator sheets.

2 Run
Dehydrate at 105°F until crunchy.

3 Ease
Label and store 1 cup of walnuts for Day 4 scrap recipe (Cucumber Hemp Seed Crackers), 2 cups of pecans for Day 4 dessert (Chocolate Orange Pie), 1 cup of pecans for Day 5 dinner (Eggplant Truffle Fettuccine), 1 cup of pecans for Day 5 scrap recipe (Hemp Seed Zucchini Pizza Crust) and 2 cups of almonds for Day 6 dessert (Banana Lemon Meringue Pie).

Almond Milk

Raw almonds, 3 cups (16 ounces), soaked 8 hours
Filtered water, 2½ cups, plus 2 additional cups

1 Prep
Drain and rinse the almonds.

2 Run
Blend the almonds with 2½ cups of water until chopped. Add 2 additional cups of water and continue to blend until creamy and thick. Pour the mixture into a milk bag, squeezing the liquid through the bag into a bowl.

3 Ease
Label and refrigerate 2 cups of milk for Day 1 lunch (Tomato Basil Soup), 3 cups of milk for Day 1 snack (Cherry Clove Smoothie) and 2 packed cups of leftover pulp in a medium storage bowl for Day 1 Scrap Bowl Recipe (Italian Flatbread). Dehydrate the remaining leftover pulp at 105°F until dry. Store in the refrigerator or freezer to be used as desired. Dried and ground nut pulp can be used to make gluten-free flour for raw cookies and cakes.

NOTE: These base recipes will be used throughout the week, but should not be made too far in advance. Please refer to the Introduction section regarding Raw Storage on page 13.

Cashew Mayonnaise

Prepare on Day 3 to use on Days 3, 4, 5 and 6.
Yields 5½ cups mayonnaise: 4½ for recipes, plus 1 cup for sandwiches

Raw cashews, 4 cups (20 ounces), soaked 2 hours
Filtered water, 2 cups
Lemon juice, ¼ cup fresh squeezed (approximately 2 lemons)
Raw apple cider vinegar, 1 tablespoon
Ground mustard powder, ½ teaspoon
Himalayan salt, 1½ teaspoons
Sweetener of choice[1], 1 teaspoon

1 Prep
Drain and rinse cashews.

2 Run
To avoid difficulty when blending large amounts, this recipe will be made in two batches. Use the spatula technique to blend half of all ingredients in a high-speed blender until creamy. Remove to a bowl. Repeat for second batch with remaining ingredients. Combine both halves in a bowl and mix well.

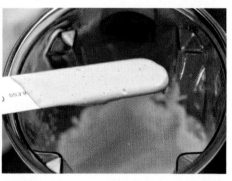

3 Ease
Label and refrigerate 1½ cups of mayonnaise for Day 3 dinner (Carrot Dill Romaine Wraps), 1½ cups mayonnaise for Day 4 dinner (Sunflower of the Sea Lemon Pate), 1 cup for Day 5 dinner (Eggplant Fennel Fettuccine) and ½ cup for Day 6 lunch (Beet Rosemary Borscht).

---

1   Choose a healthy sweetener from a local health food store or a reputable company on the Internet. My choice is raw honey or pure Grade B maple syrup, since these sweeteners are natural and easily accessible.

Brazil Nut Milk

Prepare on Day 5 to use on Day 6.
Yields 3 cups milk and 1 cup cream to make cheese

Raw Brazil nuts, 3 cups (16 ounces), soaked 4 hours
Filtered water, 2½ cups, plus 2 additional cups

1 Prep
Drain and rinse Brazil nuts.

2 Run
Use the spatula technique to blend the nuts with 2½ cups of water until smooth. Remove 1 cup blended, unstrained, thick Brazil nut cream to a glass storage bowl and set aside for Brazil Nut Cheese. Add 2 additional cups of water to the milk remaining in the blender and continue to blend the mixture until creamy. Pour the mixture into a milk bag and squeeze the liquid through the bag into a bowl. Dehydrate the remaining leftover pulp at 105°F until dry. Store in the refrigerator or freezer to be used as desired. Dried and ground nut pulp can be used to make gluten-free flour for raw cookies and cakes.

3 Ease
Label and refrigerate 1 cup of milk for Day 6 soup (Beet Rosemary Borscht) and 2 cups of milk for Day 6 smoothie (Fuji Spearmint Smoothie).

Brazil Nut Cheese

Prepare on Day 5 to use on Day 6.
Yields 1 cup

Brazil Nut Cream, 1 cup reserved
Solary Multidolphilus Powder, 1 teaspoon

1 Run
Combine the cream with the probiotic powder and mix well. Allow it to culture on the countertop for 12 hours by covering it lightly with a tea towel.

2 Ease
Label and refrigerate the cultured cheese for Day 6 dinner ('Roasted' Tomato Broccoli Pizza).

Day 1

Day 1 Outlook

Production	Tomato Reduction
Breakfast	8V Black Pepper Cocktail
Lunch	Tomato Basil Soup
Snack	Cherry Clove Smoothie + Cherry Cinnamon Candy
Dinner	Yellow Squash Tomato Pasta
Dessert	Cool Lime Raspberry Parfait
Scrap recipe	Italian Flatbread

Note: Some of today's recipes require certain ingredients to have been processed or prepared ahead of time. Plan accordingly if you are not following the book from beginning to end.

To prepare for today

1 **Make** Almond Milk in the Base Recipes for today's lunch (Tomato Basil Soup) and snack (Cherry Clove Smoothie). This recipe can be made on the previous day, if desired.

2 **Designate** a bowl for the leftover ingredients needed for the scrap recipe (Italian Flatbread).

Tomato Reduction

Yields 7 cups before reduction, 3½ cups after

Roma tomatoes, 12, seeded (reserve seeds and ribbing for 8V Black Pepper Cocktail)
Red bell peppers, 4 medium, roughly chopped
Yellow onion, ½ medium, roughly chopped
Garlic cloves, 6 medium, pressed
Cold pressed olive oil, ½ cup
Himalayan salt, 2 teaspoons

1 Run
Process the tomatoes, peppers and onion through a food processor with the slice blade. In a mixing bowl, coat the mixture with garlic, olive oil and salt.

2 Ease
Evenly distribute 2 packed cups and all of the liquid onto each of 4 solid dehydrator sheets. Dehydrate at 105°F for 3 hours. Turn trays halfway through dehydrating for balanced reduction.

Label and refrigerate 2 cups for lunch (Tomato Basil Soup) and 1½ cups for dinner (Tomato Marjoram Marinara).

8V Black Pepper Cocktail

Serves 6
Yields 2 quarts: 8 ounces per serving, plus 2 cups reserved for soup

Baby spinach, 1 package (5 ounces)
Cherry tomatoes, 3 pints
Seeds and ribbings from Tomato Reduction
Carrots, 4 medium, peeled
Cucumbers, 2 medium, sliced lengthwise
Red bell peppers, 2 medium, roughly chopped
Beet, 1 medium, peeled and roughly chopped
Parsley, 1 bunch
Celery, 8 medium stalks
YL black pepper essential oil

1 Run
Extract all ingredients except the celery and essential oil through a juicer and save the pulp for the scrap recipe. Juice the celery last to avoid celery strings in the pulp. Strain the juice for a smoother consistency, if desired. Stir to mix.

2 Ease
Label and refrigerate 2 cups of the cocktail for lunch (Tomato Basil Soup) and 1 cup of the saved pulp for the scrap recipe (Italian Flatbread).

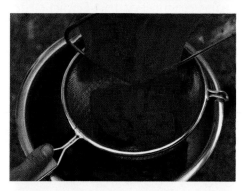

3 Presentation
Divide the cocktail into six servings. Add one drop of black pepper oil to each glass and stir when ready to serve.

Tomato Basil Soup

Serves 6
Yields 7 cups: 1 cup per serving for soup, plus 1 cup reserved for scrap recipe

8V Cocktail, 2 cups reserved
Tomato Reduction, 2 cups reserved
Almond milk, 2 cups reserved
YL basil essential oil, 2 drops

1 Run
Blend all of the ingredients in a high-speed blender until smooth.

2 Ease
Label and refrigerate 1 cup of the soup for the scrap recipe (Italian Flatbread).

3 Presentation
Divide remaining soup into 6 servings. Suggested garnish includes basil leaves, diced cucumber, tomato and avocado, drizzles of olive oil, and dashes of Italian seasoning.

Cherry Clove Smoothie

Serves 6
Yields 7 cups: 8 ounces per serving, plus 1 cup reserved for candy.

Almond milk, 3 cups
Bananas, 3 frozen
Cherries, 1 10-ounce package unsweetened frozen
YL Power Meal protein powder, 2 scoops
YL clove essential oil, 2 drops
YL cinnamon bark essential oil, 2 drops

1 Run
Blend all of the ingredients. Reserve 1 cup in blender for candy recipe (Cherry Cinnamon Candy).

2 Presentation
Divide smoothie into 6 servings.

Cherry Cinnamon Candy

Serves 6
Yields 2 cups: 4 trays or 36 pieces

Cherry Clove Smoothie, 1 cup reserved
Bananas, 2 frozen
YL cinnamon bark essential oil, 1 drop

3 Run
Blend ingredients in a high-speed blender.

4 Ease
Spoon 9 tablespoons of the candy mixture per tray onto 4 solid dehydrator sheets. Dehydrate at 105°F until disks peel. This will occur from approximately 12 to 24 hours.

5 Presentation
Form the candy into creative shapes.

Yellow Squash Tomato Pasta

Serves 6

Yellow Fennel Squash
Yields 6 cups: 1 cup per serving

Yellow squash, 6 medium
YL fennel essential oil, 2 drops
Himalayan salt, ¼ teaspoon

1 Prep
Cut the squash in half and spiral the halves with a spiralizer to resemble noodles. Cut the noodles and toss with fennel oil and salt. Set aside to make the marinara.

2 Ease
Refrigerate leftover squash pieces from spiralizer in the scrap bowl for the end of the day scrap recipe (Italian Flatbread).

Tomato Marjoram Marinara
Yields 1½ cups: ¼ cup per serving

Tomato Reduction, 1½ cups reserved
Sundried tomatoes in olive oil, ½ of 8.5-ounce jar (reserve other half for Day 5 dinner)
Medjool date, 1 pitted and soaked 10 minutes
YL marjoram essential oil, 1 drop

3 Run
Process all of the ingredients in a food processor until smooth. Then, place the mixture in a mixing bowl.

4 Ease
Refrigerate ¼ cup leftover marinara in the scrap bowl for the scrap recipe (Italian Flatbread).

5 Presentation
Top 1 cup of the squash pasta with ¼ cup of the marinara per serving. Suggested garnish includes fresh marjoram leaves.

Cool Lime Raspberry Parfait

Serves 6

Key Lime Mousse
Yields 5 cups: ½ cup per serving, plus 2 cups reserved to make Day 2 dessert

Lime zest, 2½ tablespoons (approximately 6 limes, zested)
Lime juice, 1⅓ cup fresh squeezed (approximately 8 large limes)
Sweetener of choice[1], 1 cup
Avocados, 6 medium, sliced
Himalayan salt, ¼ teaspoon

1 Run
To avoid difficulty when blending large amounts, this recipe will be made in two batches. Blend the zest, juice and sweetener in a high-speed blender until zest is blended smooth. Pour half of the mixture into a large bowl. Add the avocados and salt to the blender and complete the blending using the spatula technique. Combine both halves in the bowl and mix well.

2 Ease
Chill 3 cups of the mixture until ready to serve. Reserve 2 cups of the mousse in the blender for Day 2 dessert (Key Lime Tartlets) and make next day's dessert recipe.

Raspberry Mint Compote
Yields 2 cups: ⅓ cup per serving

Bananas, 4 fresh, diced
Raspberries, 1 12-ounce package frozen, diced
Kiwis, 6 fresh, peeled and diced
Sweetener of choice, 2 tablespoons
YL peppermint essential oil, 1 drop

3 Prep
Prepare and gently combine ingredients.

4 Presentation
Top ½ cup mousse per serving with ⅓ cup compote per serving. Suggested garnish includes mint leaves.

---

1   Choose a healthy sweetener from a local health food store or a reputable company on the Internet. My choice is raw honey or pure Grade B maple syrup, since these sweeteners are natural and easily accessible.

Italian Flatbread

Yields 5 cups batter for 2 trays bread: makes 9 sandwiches

Scrap Bowl contents (1 cup 8V pulp, 1 cup Tomato Basil Soup, leftover squash pieces, ¼ cup Tomato Marjoram Marinara)
Flaxseeds, ½ cup, ground to equal ⅔ cup flax flour
Cold pressed olive oil, 3 tablespoons
Italian seasonings, 1 tablespoon
Himalayan salt, 2 teaspoons

1 Run
Process the scrap bowl contents until they are mixed. Add the rest of the ingredients and process until smooth.

2 Ease
With an offset spatula, spread 2½ cups of the mixture onto each solid dehydrator sheet, about ¼ inch thick. Score it to make 9 bread slices per tray. Simply slide the solid sheet onto a mesh-lined dehydrator tray. Dehydrate at 105°F for 3 hours. Take out each tray and add a mesh tray to the top. Flip the tray over onto the mesh, peel off the dehydrator sheet, place it back in the dehydrator and continue until dry for approximately 6 hours.

3 Presentation
Use the bread to make vegetable sandwiches with Day 2 lunch (Thai Lemongrass Soup).

Day 2

Day 2 Outlook

Production	Red Pepper Reduction
Breakfast	Citrus Ginger Splash
Lunch	Thai Lemongrass Soup
Snack	Strawberry Grapefruit Smoothie + Strawberry Grapefruit Candy
Dinner	Nori Red Pepper Hand Rolls
Dessert	Key Lime Tartlet
Scrap recipe	Sunflower Nori Crisps

Note: Some of today's recipes require certain ingredients to have been processed or prepared ahead of time. Plan accordingly if you are not following the book from beginning to end.

To prepare for today

1 Soak 1 cup of sunflower seeds for 8 hours for today's scrap recipe (Sunflower Nori Crisps).

2 Open a total of 4 young coconuts to yield 2 packed cups coconut meat for today's lunch (Thai Lemongrass Soup) and snack (Strawberry Grapefruit Smoothie). See Opening a Young Coconut on page 50.

3 Designate a bowl for the leftover ingredients needed for the scrap recipe (Sunflower Nori Crisps).

To prepare for Day 3

4 If desired, the Cashew Mayonnaise for Day 3 may be prepared today. See Base Recipes for details.

Red Pepper Reduction

Yields 8 cups before reduction, 4 cups after

Red bell peppers, 6 medium
Carrots, 5 medium, peeled
Yellow onion, ½ medium, peeled
Ginger, 2 tablespoons, grated
Garlic cloves, 6 medium, pressed
Raw sesame oil, ½ cup
Nama Shoyu, wheat-free Tamari or raw coconut aminos, ½ cup
Toasted sesame oil, ¼ cup

1 Run
Process the peppers, carrots and onions through a food processor with the slice blade. In a mixing bowl, coat the mixture with the remaining ingredients.

2 Ease
Evenly distribute 2 packed cups and all of the liquid onto each of 4 solid dehydrator sheets. Dehydrate at 105°F for 3 hours. Turn trays halfway through dehydrating for balanced reduction.

Label and refrigerate 2 cups of reduction for lunch (Thai Lemongrass Soup) and 2 cups for dinner (Red Pepper Paste).

Opening A Young Coconut

1 Shave the top part of the coconut with a cleaver. Lay it sideways shaving away from yourself towards the end until the brown part is revealed. Continue to turn the coconut until all sides of the top have been done.

2 Puncture the top part of the coconut. Place the coconut right-side up, lift the cleaver and carefully hit the top side of the coconut with the heel of the cleaver making sure to imbed the cleaver into the top of the coconut. The 'lid' should easily pry open to create a nice round opening since the top has been shaved. Gently bend the cleaver to crack the top open.

3 Pour out the coconut water with a strainer atop a pitcher to catch any wood debris.

4 Split the coconut in half using the cleaver. Lift the cleaver and forcefully make contact with coconut through the middle. The cleaver will not make it all the way through and hopefully should get stuck. Try again if the cleaver does not get stuck the first time. Then, lift the cleaver with the coconut attached and pound the coconut on the cutting board until it splits open.

5 Using a firm rubber spatula, scoop the coconut meat out of both halves of the coconut. The spatula is preferred to remove the meat from the shell rather than a spoon because a spoon will scoop too much of the wood under the meat making the cleaning process more tedious.

6 Clean the coconut meat with a paring knife, removing all of the wood residue to avoid any hard particles in the recipe. However, if a little gets into the mixture, it will blend up in the Vita Mix. Just be conscious of getting it clean. It is not necessary to rinse the coconut, as using water takes more of the meat away.

7 Store the coconut meat and coconut water separately to use in recipes. The coconut water can be infused with the essential oils for a refreshing drink and will remain fresh for two or three days.

Citrus Ginger Splash

Serves 6
Yields 2 quarts: 8 ounces per serving, plus 1 cup reserved for soup

Valencia oranges, 12 medium, halved
Grapefruit, 4 medium, halved
Lemons, 2 medium, halved
Limes, 2 large, halved
YL ginger, lemon, orange and grapefruit essential oils

1 Run
Use a citrus juicer to juice the fruit. Strain the juice for a smoother consistency, if desired. Stir to mix.

2 Ease
Reserve 1 cup of juice for lunch (Thai Lemongrass Soup).

3 Presentation
Divide the juice into six servings. Add two drops of each essential oil to each glass and stir when ready to serve.

Thai Lemongrass Soup

Serves 6
Yields 6 cups: 1 cup per serving

Young coconut water, 2 cups (approximately 2 coconuts)
Young coconut meat, 1 packed cup (approximately 2 coconuts)
Citrus Splash, 1 cup reserved
Red Pepper Reduction, 2 cups reserved
YL lemongrass essential oil, 2 drops

1 Run
Blend all of the ingredients in a high-speed blender until semi-smooth.

2 Presentation
Divide soup into six servings. Suggested garnish includes shredded Napa cabbage, minced Thai basil, diced scallions and/or drizzles of toasted sesame oil. Serve with Italian Flatbread sandwiches from Day 1.

Strawberry Grapefruit Smoothie

Serves 6
Yields 7 cups smoothie: 8 ounces per serving, plus 1 cup reserved for candy

Young coconut water, 2½ cups (approximately 3 coconuts)
Young coconut meat, 1 packed cup (approximately 2 coconuts)
Strawberries, 1 12-ounce package frozen
YL Power Meal protein powder, 2 scoops
Bananas, 3 frozen
YL grapefruit essential oil

1 Run
Blend all of the ingredients, except essential oil. Reserve 1 cup in the blender for the candy recipe (Strawberry Grapefruit Candy).

2 Presentation
Divide smoothie into six servings. Add three drops of grapefruit oil to each glass and stir when ready to serve.

Strawberry Grapefruit Candy

Serves 6
Yields 2 cups: 4 trays or 36 pieces

Strawberry Grapefruit Smoothie,
1 cup reserved
Banana, 1 frozen
YL grapefruit essential oil, 2 drops

3 Run
Blend all of the ingredients in a high-speed blender.

4 Ease
Spoon 9 tablespoons of the candy mixture per tray onto 4 solid dehydrator sheets. Dehydrate at 105°F until disks peel. This will occur from approximately 12 to 24 hours.

5 Presentation
Form the candy into creative shapes.

Nori Red Pepper Hand Rolls

Serves 6: 4 rolls per serving

Coconut Ginger Rice

Yields 2 cups rice: ¼ cup per serving, plus ½ cup reserved for scrap recipe

Coconut flakes, 1 cup, dried
Pine nuts, ⅓ cup, not soaked
Cauliflower florets, 1 medium head, chopped fine
Himalayan salt, ½ teaspoon
YL ginger oil, 6 drops

1 Run
Process the coconut flakes and pine nuts in a food processor until crumbly. Add the cauliflower until the texture of the mixture resembles rice. Add the salt and ginger oil and mix well. Set aside to make the paste.

2 Ease
Store ½ cup of rice in the scrap bowl for the end of the day scrap recipe (Sunflower Nori Crisps).

Red Pepper Paste

Yields 2 cups paste: ¼ cup per serving, plus ½ cup reserved for scrap recipe

Red Pepper Reduction, 2 cups reserved
Nama Shoyu, wheat-free Tamari or raw coconut aminos, 2 tablespoons
Thai Kitchen red curry paste, 2 tablespoons
YL black pepper essential oil, 4 drops

3 Run
Process Red Pepper Paste ingredients in a food processor until almost smooth.

4 Ease
Store ½ cup paste in the scrap bowl for the end of the day scrap recipe (Sunflower Nori Crisps).

Nori Red Pepper Hand Rolls

Coconut Ginger Rice
Red Pepper Paste
Avocados, 2 medium, sliced
Nori sheets, 6 dried, quartered
Sprouts, 1 pint of choice

5 Presentation
Cut Nori into quarters to form 4 squares. Spread each square with 1 tablespoon each of rice and paste. Arrange 2 slices of avocados with a few sprout sprigs on top and fold corners from opposite sides. Garnish each roll with tie wraps made from chives. Optional: Chard or other lettuce leaf can replace Nori sheets.

Key Lime Tartlet

Serves 6

Key Lime Tartlet Filling
Yields 2½ cups pie filling: ⅓ cup per tart

Key Lime Mousse, 2 cups reserved
Virgin coconut oil, ½ cup

1 Run
Blend reserved Key Lime Mousse with coconut oil in a high-speed blender. Set aside to make the crust.

Macadamia Coconut Crust
Yields 1 cup crust: 2½ tablespoons per tart for 6 3½-inch tartlet tins

Coconut flakes, 1 cup dried
Macadamia nuts, 1 cup (6 ounces), not soaked
Sweetener of choice[1], 1 tablespoon
Himalayan salt, ½ teaspoon

2 Run
Grind the coconut in a food processor until fine. Add Macadamia nuts and mix until the mixture is a semi-butter texture. Be careful not to process it into a smooth cream. Add the sweetener and salt and combine until mix sticks together. Remove to a mixing bowl and chill in the refrigerator for 1 hour.

3 Ease
Prepare each tartlet tin by pressing plastic wrap around the inside before forming the crust. This is a simple way to release the tartlet from the small tin after it has been frozen. Press 2½ tablespoons of crust into the bottom of 6 3½-inch tartlet tins. Pour ⅓ cup filling into each tartlet. Wrap a cookie sheet in plastic wrap, and place the tartlets on the sheet. Cover the sheet with plastic wrap and place it in the freezer.

4 Presentation
When ready to eat, remove tartlets from the freezer and tins.

---

1   My choice is raw honey or pure Grade B maple syrup, since these sweeteners are natural and easily accessible.

Sunflower Nori Crisps

Severs 6: 12 pieces per serving
Yields 2 cups of pate for 4 Nori sheets: ½ cup of pate per sheet for 18 triangles

Scrap Bowl contents (½ cup Ginger Rice, ½ cup Red Pepper Paste)
Sunflower seeds, 1 cup, soaked 8 hours
Chickpea miso, 1 tablespoon
Five-spice powder, 1 teaspoon
Nori sheets, 4 untoasted dried
Sesame seeds, 2 tablespoons

1 Prep
Drain and rinse the sunflower seeds.

2 Run
Process the scrap bowl contents, sunflower seeds, miso and Chinese Five Spice in a food processor until it resembles the texture of pate.

3 Ease
Spread ½ cup of pate onto each Nori sheet and gently transfer it to a mesh-lined dehydrator tray. Sprinkle with ½ tablespoon of sesame seeds per sheet. Dehydrate at 105°F until dry, or approximately 8 to 12 hours. Cut each Nori into 9 squares. Cut the squares into triangles, and label and store them for future use.

4 Presentation
Serve with Day 3 lunch (Carrot Coriander Soup).

Day 3

Day 3 Outlook

Production	Carrot Reduction
Breakfast	Carrot Orange Milk
Lunch	Carrot Coriander Soup
Snack	Orange Cinnamon Smoothie + Pear Cinnamon Candy
Dinner	Carrot Dill Romaine Wraps
Dessert	Caramel Orange Banana Parfait
Scrap recipe	Pecan Carrot Bread

Note: Some of today's recipes require certain ingredients to have been processed or prepared ahead of time. Plan accordingly if you are not following the book from beginning to end.

To prepare for today

1 **Soak** 1 cup (4 ounces) of pecans for 4 hours to be split between snack (Orange Cinnamon Smoothie) and scrap recipe (Pecan Carrot Bread).

2 **Soak** ¼ cup of pine nuts for 2 hours for dessert (Caramel Orange Banana Parfait). Pit 12 plump Medjool dates for dessert (Caramel Orange Banana Parfait).

3 **Make** Cashew Mayonnaise. Optional: This recipe can be made on the previous day, if desired. See Base Recipes for details.

4 **Designate** a bowl for the leftover ingredients needed for the scrap recipe (Pecan Carrot Bread).

Carrot Reduction

Yields: 8 cups before reduction, 4 cups after

Celery, 4 medium stalks
Carrots, 1 bag (2 pounds) or 13 medium, peeled
Yellow onion, ½ medium, roughly chopped
Grapeseed oil, ½ cup
Raw apple cider vinegar, 1 tablespoon
Himalayan salt, ½ tablespoon

1 Run
Process the celery, carrots and onion through a food processor with the slice blade. In a mixing bowl, coat the mixture with the remaining ingredients.

2 Ease
Evenly distribute 2 packed cups and all of the liquid onto each of 4 solid dehydrator sheets with mesh-lined trays. Dehydrate at 105°F for 3 hours. Turn trays halfway through dehydrating for balanced reduction.

Label and refrigerate 2 cups for lunch (Carrot Coriander Bisque), 1 cup for dinner (Carrot Dill Pate) and add 1 cup to the scrap bowl for scrap recipe (Pecan Carrot Bread).

Carrot Orange Milk

Serves 6
Yields 2 quarts: 8 ounces per serving, plus 2 cups reserved

Carrots, 1 bag (10 pounds), peeled
YL orange oil

1 Run
Extract the carrots through a juicer and save the pulp for the scrap recipe. Strain the juice for a smoother consistency, if desired. Stir to mix.

2 Ease
Label and refrigerate 2 cups juice for lunch (Carrot Coriander Soup) and 2 cups of the pulp for dinner (Carrot Dill Romaine Wraps). Add 1 cup of leftover pulp to the scrap bowl for the scrap recipe (Pecan Carrot Bread). Dehydrate the remaining leftover pulp at 105°F until dry. Store it in airtight containers to be used as desired. Dried and ground carrot pulp can be used to make gluten- free flour for raw cookies and cakes.

3 Presentation
Divide juice into six servings. Add 2 drops of YL orange essential oil to each glass and stir when ready to serve.

Carrot Coriander Soup

Serves 6
Yields 6 cups: 1 cup per serving

Carrot Reduction, 2 packed cups reserved
Carrot Milk, 2 cups reserved
Filtered water, 3 cups
Ground cumin, 1 tablespoon
Himalayan salt, 1 teaspoon
Avocado, 1, sliced
YL coriander essential oil, 1 drop

1 Run
Blend the Carrot Reduction, carrot milk, water, cumin and salt in a high-speed blender until smooth. Store 1 cup of the soup in the scrap bowl for the scrap recipe (Pecan Carrot Bread). Add avocado and coriander oil to the blender and mix.

2 Presentation
Divide into six servings. Suggested garnish includes diced cucumber, tomato, drizzles of olive oil and dashes of ground cumin. Serve with the Sunflower Nori Crisps from Day 2.

Orange Cinnamon Smoothie

Serves 6
Yields 7 cups: 8 ounces per serving, plus 1 cup reserved for candy.

Orange juice, 3 cups fresh squeezed (approximately 4-pound bag or 11 Valencia oranges)
Bananas, 3 frozen
Pears, 2 medium, peeled
Pecans, 1 cup soaked (½ cup dry pecans before soaked)
YL Power Meal protein powder, 2 scoops
YL cinnamon bark essential oil, 3 drops

1 Run
Blend all of the ingredients, adding the oil last to allow it to mix throughout.
Reserve 1 cup in the blender for the candy recipe (Pear Cinnamon Candy).

2 Presentation
Divide smoothie into six servings.

Pear Cinnamon Candy

Serves 6
Yields 2 cups: 4 trays or 36 pieces

Orange Cinnamon Smoothie, 1 cup reserved
Banana, 1 frozen
Pear, 1 medium, peeled
YL cinnamon bark essential oil, 1 drop

3 Run
Blend all of the ingredients in a high-speed blender.

4 Ease
Spoon 9 tablespoons of the candy mixture per tray onto 4 solid dehydrator sheets. Dehydrate at 105°F until disks peel. This will occur from approximately 12 to 24 hours.

5 Presentation
Form the candy into creative shapes.

Carrot Dill Romaine Wraps

Serves 6
Yields 2 wraps per serving

Carrot Dill Pate

Yields 2¼ cups pate: 3 tablespoons per wrap, 2 wraps per person

Carrot Reduction, 1 cup reserved
Cashew Mayonnaise, 1 cup reserved (see Base Recipes)
Carrot pulp from juice, 1 cup reserved
Garlic cloves, 2 medium, pressed
Ginger, 1 tablespoon grated
YL dill essential oil, 3 drops
Romaine hearts, 12

1 Run
Process the Carrot Reduction and Cashew Mayonnaise in a food processor until smooth. Add remaining ingredients and process until the texture resembles pate.

2 Presentation
Fill each Romaine heart with 3 tablespoons of pate and set aside. Make the Caper Lemon Sauce.

Caper Lemon Sauce

Yields ¾ cup sauce, 1 tablespoon per serving

Cashew Mayonnaise, ½ cup reserved (see Base Recipes)
YL lemon essential oil, 4 drops
Capers, 1 3.5-ounces jar, drained

3 Presentation
Combine all of the ingredients. Drizzle 1 tablespoon of sauce on top of each wrap. Suggested garnish includes minced dill.

Caramel Orange Banana Parfait

Serves 6

Caramel Orange Cream
Yields 3½ cups, ¼ cup per serving, plus 2 cups to make Day 4 dessert

Medjool dates, 12 plump, pitted
Orange juice, ¼ cup fresh squeezed
(approximately 1 Valencia orange)
Young coconut meat, 2 packed cups
(approximately 4 coconuts)
Pine nuts, ¼ cup soaked
Virgin coconut oil, 3 tablespoons
Pears, 2 medium, peeled
YL orange essential oil, 10 drops
Himalayan salt, ⅛ teaspoon

Banana Nutmeg Compote
Yields 3 cups: ½ cup per serving

Bananas, 3 fresh, diced
Pears, 2 medium, peeled and diced
Sweetener of choice[1], 2 tablespoons
Ground cinnamon, 2 teaspoons
Vanilla flavoring, 1 teaspoon
YL nutmeg essential oil, 2 drops

1 Prep
Pour the orange juice over the pitted dates and baste them to soften, approximately 10 minutes. Drain and rinse pine nuts.

2 Run
Using the spatula technique, blend all of the ingredients in a high-speed blender until creamy.

3 Ease
Chill 1½ cups of the cream until ready to serve. Reserve 2 cups of cream in the blender for Day 4 dessert (Chocolate Orange Pie) and make next day's dessert recipe.

4 Prep
Gently combine ingredients.

5 Presentation
Divide the compote into ½ cup servings and top with ¼ cup Caramel Orange Cream. Suggested garnish includes sprinkles of cinnamon, orange zest and sliced bananas.

---

1   My choice is raw honey or pure Grade B maple syrup, since these sweeteners are natural and easily accessible.

Pecan Carrot Bread

Yields 5 cups batter for 2 trays bread: makes 9 sandwiches

Pecans, 1 cup soaked (½ cup before soaked)
Scrap Bowl contents (1 cup Carrot Orange Milk pulp, 1 cup Carrot Coriander Soup)
Filtered water, ¼ cup
Flaxseeds, ½ cup, ground to equal ⅔ cup flax flour
Cold pressed olive oil, 3 Tablespoons
Himalayan salt, 1 teaspoon

1 Prep
Drain and rinse the pecans.

2 Run
Grind the pecans in a food processor. Add the scrap bowl contents and water and process until the texture resembles pate. Add the remaining ingredients and process until it is semi-smooth.

3 Ease
With an offset spatula, spread 2½ cups of the mixture onto each solid dehydrator sheet, about ¼ inch thick. Score it to make 9 bread slices per tray or use special cutters for a variety of shapes and sizes to serve as an hors d'oeuvre. Simply slide the solid sheet onto a mesh-lined dehydrator tray. Dehydrate at 105°F for 2 hours. Flip onto mesh and continue until dry for approximately 6 hours.

4 Presentation
Use the bread to make vegetable sandwiches or garnish cut-out shapes for hors d'oeuvres with Day 4 lunch (Cucumber Tarragon Soup).

Day 4

Day 4 Outlook

Production Cucumber Reduction
Breakfast Cucumber Dill Tonic
Lunch Cucumber Tarragon Soup
Snack Green Tangerine Smoothie + Pineapple Tangerine Candy
Dinner Sunflower of the Sea Lemon Pate
Dessert Chocolate Orange Pie
Scrap recipe Cucumber Hemp Seed Crackers

Note: Some of today's recipes require certain ingredients to have been processed or prepared ahead of time. Plan accordingly if you are not following the book from beginning to end.

To prepare for today

1 **Soak** 1 cup (5 ounces) of sunflower seeds for 8 hours for dinner (Sunflower of the Sea Lemon Pate).

2 **Soak** 1 cup (5 ounces) of cashews for 2 to 4 hours for lunch (Cucumber Tarragon Soup).

3 **Designate** a bowl for the leftover ingredients needed for the scrap recipe (Cucumber Hemp Seed Crackers).

Cucumber Reduction

Yields 12 cups before reduction, 6 cups after

Cucumbers, 10 large, peeled and seeded (reserve seeds and ribbing)
Grapeseed oil, ½ cup
Raw apple cider vinegar, 2 tablespoons
Himalayan salt, 2 teaspoons

1 Prep
Quarter the cucumber and add leftover seeds and ribbing to the tonic juicing.

2 Run
Slice cucumbers through a food processor with the slice blade. Remove to a mixing bowl. Coat with the oil, vinegar and salt.

3 Ease
Evenly distribute 2 packed cups and all of the liquid onto each of 6 solid dehydrator sheets. Dehydrate at 105°F for 3 hours. Turn trays halfway through dehydrating for balanced reduction.

Store 4 cups for lunch (Cucumber Tarragon Soup), 1 cup for dinner (Sunflower of the Sea Lemon Pate), and add 1 cup to the scrap bowl for scrap recipe (Cucumber Hemp Seed Crackers).

Cucumber Dill Tonic

Serves 6
Yields 2 quarts: 8 ounces per serving, plus 2 cups reserved for soup and smoothie.

Cucumbers, 3 large
Reserved seeds and ribbing from Cucumber Reduction
Green apples, 3 medium, sliced
Rainbow chard, 1 head
Lacinato kale, 1 head
Romaine lettuce, 1 head
Celery, 1 bunch
YL dill essential oil

1 Run
Extract the cucumbers, apples, chard, kale and romaine through a juicer and save the pulp for the dinner pate recipe. Juice the celery last to avoid celery strings in the pulp. Strain the juice for a smoother consistency, if desired. Stir to mix.

2 Ease
Store 1 cup of the juice for lunch (Cucumber Tarragon Soup), 1 cup of juice for the smoothie recipe (Green Tangerine Smoothie) and ½ cup of the saved pulp for dinner (Sunflower of the Sea Lemon Pate).

3 Presentation
Divide the juice into 6 servings. Add 1 drop dill essential oil to each glass and stir when ready to serve.

Cucumber Tarragon Soup

Serves 6
Yields 6 cups: 1 cup per serving

Cucumber Reduction, 4 cups reserved
Cucumber Tonic, 1 cup reserved
Filtered water, 1 cup
Cashews, 1 cup (5 ounces), soaked 2 hours
Himalayan salt, ½ teaspoon
YL tarragon essential oil, 1 drop

1 Run
Blend all of the ingredients in a high-speed blender until smooth.

2 Presentation
Divide the soup into six servings. Suggested garnish includes diced tomato, cucumber, avocado, and/ or drizzles of olive oil and sprinkles of spirulina. Serve with Pecan Carrot Bread from Day 3 (see page 73).

Green Tangerine Smoothie

Serves 6
Yields 7 cups smoothie: 8 ounces per serving, plus 1 cup reserved for candy

Tangerine juice, 2½ cups fresh squeezed (approximately 9 large tangerines)
Cucumber Tonic, 1 cup reserved
Bananas, 3 frozen
Pineapple, ½ 16-ounce package frozen
YL Power Meal protein powder, 2 scoops
YL tangerine essential oil

1 Run
Blend all of the ingredients, except the essential oil. Reserve 1 cup in the blender for the candy recipe (Pineapple Tangerine Candy).

2 Presentation
Divide the smoothie into six servings. Add 1 drop tangerine essential oil to each glass and stir when ready to serve.

Pineapple Tangerine Candy

Serves 6
Yields 2 cups: 3 trays or 36 pieces

Green Tangerine Smoothie, 1 cup reserved
Banana, 1 frozen
Pineapple, ½ 16-ounce package frozen
YL tangerine essential oil, 2 drops

1 Run
Blend all of the ingredients in a high-speed blender.

2 Ease
Spoon 9 tablespoons of the candy mixture onto each of 4 solid dehydrator sheets. Dehydrate at 105°F until disks peel. This will occur from approximately 12 to 24 hours.

3 Presentation
Form the candy into creative shapes.

Sunflower of the Sea Lemon Pate

Serves 6
Yields 4 cups pate, ⅔ cup per serving

Sunflower seeds, 1 cup (5 ounces), soaked 8 hours
Cucumber Reduction, 1 cup reserved
Cashew Mayonnaise, 1 cup, plus ½ cup reserved
Cucumber Dill Tonic pulp, ½ cup reserved
Himalayan salt, 1 teaspoon
Dulse, ¼ cup minced (cut with kitchen scissors)
YL lemon essential oil, 2 drops
Green apple, 1 medium, diced with skins
Celery, 3 medium stalks, diced
Red onion, ¼ medium, minced

1 Run
Process sunflower seeds, Cucumber Reduction, 1 cup of the Cashew Mayonnaise, Cucumber Dill Tonic pulp and salt in a food processor until the texture resembles pate. Add dulse and lemon oil and pulse until flakes mix throughout. Remove to a bowl and add the apple, celery and onion.

2 Presentation
Divide the pate into ⅔ cup mounds and top each with approximately 1 tablespoon per serving from the ½ cup of reserved mayonnaise. Suggested garnish includes a bed of fresh herb salad, hollowed tomatoes and dashes of black pepper.

Chocolate Orange Pie

Serves 6

Chocolate Orange Pie Filling
Yields 4 cups

Caramel Orange Cream, 2 cups reserved
Raw cacao powder or roasted carob powder, 1 cup
Grade B maple syrup, ¾ cup
Virgin coconut oil or dehydrator-melted cacao butter, ½ cup
YL orange essential oil, 20 drops
Nama Shoyu, wheat-free Tamari or raw coconut aminos, ½ teaspoon

1 Run
Blend all of the ingredients in a high-speed blender. Set aside to make the crust.

Orange Cinnamon Compote
Serves 6
Yields 2 cups: ⅓ cup per serving

Navel oranges, 6 sectioned with no pith or membranes
Bananas, 3 fresh, diced
Sweetener of choice[1], 1 tablespoon
YL cinnamon bark essential oil, 1 drop

4 Prep
Gently combine all of the ingredients.

5 Presentation
When ready to eat, remove the Chocolate Orange Pie from the freezer and springform pan. Top each pie slice with ⅓ cup compote per serving. Suggested garnish includes sprinkles of ground cinnamon and 3 drops of orange oil.

Pecan Cranberry Crust
Yields 1½ cups to fill a 7-inch springform pan

Pecans, 2 cups, soaked and dehydrated
Dried cranberries, 1 cup (juice-sweetened)
Himalayan salt, ½ teaspoon

2 Run
Grind all of the ingredients until the texture resembles meal.

3 Ease
Press the mixture into the bottom of a round 7-inch springform pan. Pour Chocolate Orange Pie Filling evenly into crust. Cover and freeze until firm.

---

1   My choice is raw honey or pure Grade B maple syrup, since these sweeteners are natural and easily accessible.

Cucumber Hemp Seed Crackers

Serves 6
Yields 1½ cups batter: 24 rectangle crackers for 4 crackers per serving

Cucumber Reduction, 1 cup reserved
Walnuts, 1 cup soaked and dehydrated
Flaxseeds, 2 tablespoons, ground to equal 3 packed tablespoons flax flour
Hemp seeds, ¼ cup, not soaked

1 Run
Grind the walnuts in a food processor until the texture resembles meal. Add all of the ingredients and mix until it is even throughout. Remove to a mixing bowl.

2 Ease
With an offset spatula, spread 1½ cups of the mixture onto a solid dehydrator sheet with mesh-lined tray, about ⅛ inch thick. Score into 24 rectangle crackers (6 rows by 4 rows). Dehydrate at 105°F for 2 hours. Flip onto mesh and continue until dry for approximately 6 hours.

3 Presentation
Serve with Day 5 lunch (Zucchini Sage Bisque).

Day 5

Day 5 Outlook

Production	Zucchini and Eggplant Reduction
Breakfast	Lavender Ginger Lemonade
Lunch	Zucchini Sage Bisque
Snack	Blueberry Lemon Smoothie + Blueberry Banana Candy
Dinner	Eggplant Truffle Fettuccine
Dessert	Coconut Blueberry Parfait
Scrap recipe	Hemp Seed Zucchini Pizza Crust

Note: Some of today's recipes require certain ingredients to have been processed or prepared ahead of time. Plan accordingly if you are not following the book from beginning to end.

To prepare for today

1 **Soak** 1¾ cup (9 ounces) of pine nuts for 2 hours to be split between lunch (Zucchini Sage Bisque), snack (Blueberry Lemon Smoothie) and dinner (Eggplant Truffle Fettuccine).

2 **Open** 6 young coconuts to yield 3 packed cups of coconut meat for dessert (Coconut Lemon Whip).

3 **Designate** a bowl for the leftover ingredients needed for the scrap recipe (Hemp Seed Zucchini Pizza Crust).

To prepare for coming days

4 **Make** Brazil Nut Milk for Day 6 lunch (Beet Rosemary Borscht) and snack (Fuji Spearmint Smoothie). See Base Recipes for details.

5 **Make** Brazil Nut Cheese for Day 6 dinner ('Roasted' Tomato Broccoli Pizza). See Base Recipes for details.

Zucchini and Eggplant Reduction

Yields 10 cups zucchini before reduction, 5 cups after
Yields 4 cups eggplant before reduction, 2 cups after

Eggplant, 2 medium, peeled, sliced with a mandolin and finely diced
Himalayan salt, 1 tablespoon
Zucchini, 10 medium, peeled and quartered
Celery, 4 medium stalks
Yellow onion, 1 small, ½ sliced and ½ finely diced
Garlic cloves, 8 pressed and divided
Cold pressed olive oil, ¼ cup, plus ½ additional cup
Himalayan salt, 2 teaspoons, divided

1 Prep
To organize this day's double reduction production, begin with labeling two bowls: eggplant and zucchini. Sprinkle the eggplant with salt and rest in a colander for 20 minutes to remove any bitterness. Rinse the eggplant well and remove to the eggplant bowl.

2 Run
Coat the eggplant with the finely diced onion, 4 cloves of garlic, ¼ cup of olive oil and 1 teaspoon of salt. Slice the zucchini, celery and ½ sliced onion through a food processor with a slice blade. Remove to the zucchini bowl and coat with the remaining 4 cloves of garlic, ½ cup of olive oil and 1 teaspoon of salt.

3 Ease
Evenly distribute 2 packed cups of the zucchini mixture onto each of 5 solid dehydrator sheets. Distribute eggplant mix evenly onto 2 solid dehydrator sheets. Dehydrate at 105°F for 3 hours. Turn trays halfway through dehydrating for balanced reduction.

Label and store 3 cups of the Zucchini Reduction for soup and 1 cup in the scrap bowl for scrap recipe (Hemp Seed Zucchini Pizza Crust). Refrigerate the Eggplant Reduction for dinner (Eggplant Truffle Fettuccine).

Lavender Ginger Lemonade

Serves 6
Yields 8½ cups: 8 ounces per serving, plus 2½ cups reserved for smoothie

Purple or red grapes, 3 pounds
Green and/or Fuji apples, 8 medium
Celery, 4 medium stalks
Lemons, 4 medium, quartered with rind
Ginger, 1 inch (1 ounce) with peel
YL lavender essential oil, 2 drops
YL lemon essential oil
YL ginger essential oil

1 Run
Extract grapes, apples, celery, lemons and ginger through a juicer. Stir to mix.

2 Ease
Label and refrigerate 2½ cups of juice for smoothie recipe (Blueberry Lemon Smoothie).

3 Presentation
Add lavender oil to the batch. Stir to mix. Divide juice into six servings. Add 2 drops each of lemon and ginger oil to each glass and stir when ready to serve.

Optional: This juice can be made without grapes, if organic cannot be found. Increase apples to 16 and use 8 green and 8 Fuji apples.

Variation: This juice can be diluted with filtered water or organic green tea, served over crushed ice and sipped throughout the day.

Zucchini Sage Bisque

Serves 6
Yields 7 cups: 1 cup per serving, plus ½ cup reserved for Hemp Seed Zucchini Pizza Crust

Zucchini Reduction, 4 cups reserved
Filtered water, 2 cups
Pine nuts, ½ cup, soaked
Himalayan salt, 1½ teaspoons
YL sage essential oil, 1 drop

1 Prep
Drain and rinse pine nuts. Blend all of the ingredients in a high-speed blender until smooth.

2 Ease
Add ½ cup of the soup to the scrap bowl for scrap recipe (Hemp Seed Zucchini Pizza Crust).

3 Presentation
Divide the remaining soup into six servings. Suggested garnish includes diced celery, tomato and purple onion, drizzles of olive oil and fresh minced sage. Serve with the Cucumber Hemp Seed Crackers from Day 4.

Blueberry Lemon Smoothie

Serves 6
Yields 7 cups smoothie: 8 ounces per serving, plus 1 cup reserved for candy

Lemonade, 2½ cups reserved
Pine nuts, ½ cup, soaked
Blueberries, 1 8-ounce package frozen
Bananas, 3 frozen
YL Power Meal protein powder, 2 scoops
YL lemon essential oil

1 Prep
Drain and rinse pine nuts.

2 Run
Blend all of the ingredients, except the essential oil. Reserve 1 cup in the blender for the candy recipe (Blueberry Banana Candy).

3 Presentation
Divide the smoothie into six servings. Add 2 drops lemon essential oil to each glass and stir when ready to serve.

Blueberry Banana Candy

Serves 6
Yields 2 cups: 4 trays or 36 pieces

Blueberry Lemon Smoothie, 1 cup reserved
Bananas, 2 frozen
YL lemon essential oil, 1 drop

1 Run
Blend all of the ingredients in a high-speed blender.

2 Ease
Spoon 9 tablespoons of the candy mixture onto each of 4 solid dehydrator sheets. Dehydrate at 105°F until disks peel. This will occur from approximately 12 to 24 hours.

3 Presentation
Form the candy into creative shapes.

Eggplant Truffle Fettuccine

Serves 6

Eggplant Fennel Sausage
Yields 2 cups pate

Pecans, 1 cup, soaked and dehydrated
Pine nuts, ¼ cup, not soaked
Dulse, 1 packed tablespoon whole
Eggplant Reduction, all reserved
Nama Shoyu, wheat-free Tamari or raw coconut aminos,
1 tablespoon
Anise seed, 2 teaspoons whole
Sage, 1 teaspoon minced, fresh or dried
YL fennel oil, 2 drops

1 Run
Process the pecans, pine nuts and dulse in a food processor until the texture resembles meal. Add the remaining ingredients and pulse chop until it is mixed throughout. Be careful not to over-process the eggplant, which can become bitter.

2 Ease
Sprinkle onto 2 solid dehydrator sheets to resemble the texture of sausage. Dehydrate at 105°F until crusted on the outside and moist on the inside or approximately 1 to 2 hours. Make the Alfredo and fettuccine noodles.

Pine Nut Truffle Alfredo
Yields 1 ¼ cup

Cashew Mayonnaise, 1 cup
Pine nuts, ¾ cup, soaked
Garlic clove, 1 pressed
Onion flakes, 1 tablespoon dried
Raw apple cider vinegar, 1 teaspoon
White truffle oil, 1 tablespoon
Himalayan salt, 1 teaspoon

3 Prep
Drain and rinse pine nuts.

4 Run
Blend all of the ingredients in a high-speed blender until creamy. The sauce should be thick. Set aside to make fettuccine.

Eggplant Truffle Fettuccine
Serves 6

Zucchini, 6 medium
Pine Nut Truffle Alfredo
Sundried tomatoes from Day 1,
(½ of 8.5-ounce jar, diced with oil)
Eggplant Fennel Sausage

5 Prep
Slice the zucchini into thin strips (1/16" to 1/8") lengthwise using a mandolin. If the strips tear, they are too thin. Stack the strips and cut off the peel. Slice the strips into ½ inch wide noodles using a chef knife. Combine noodles with sundried tomatoes and toss with Alfredo sauce.

6 Presentation
Divide into six equal servings. Sprinkle the eggplant sausage on top. Suggested garnish includes dashes of ground pepper and fennel leaves.

Coconut Blueberry Parfait

Serves 6

Coconut Lemon Whip
Yields 6 cups: ⅓ cup per serving, plus 4 cups reserved for Banana Lemon Meringue Pie

Young coconut meat, 4 packed cups (approximately 8 young coconuts)
Lemon juice, ⅓ cup fresh squeezed (approximately 5 medium lemons)
Sweetener of choice[1], ⅓ cup
Virgin coconut oil, ⅓ cup
Almond flavoring, 2 tablespoons
Himalayan salt, ½ teaspoon
YL lemon essential oil, 6 drops

1 Run
To avoid difficulty when blending large amounts, this recipe will be made in two batches.   Using the spatula technique, blend half of all the ingredients in a high-speed blender until creamy. Remove to a bowl. Repeat for second batch with remaining ingredients. Combine both halves and mix well.

2 Ease
Chill 2 cups until ready to serve. Refrigerate the remaining whip for Day 6 dessert (Banana Lemon Meringue Pie). Make the first part of Day 6 dessert: the crust (Banana Lemon Crust) and the pie filling (Banana Lemon Meringue Pie Filling).

Blueberry Lemon Compote
Yields 3 cups, ½ cup per serving

Bananas, 4 fresh, diced
Blueberries, 1 8-ounce package frozen
Sweetener of choice, 2 tablespoons
YL lemon essential oil, 6 drops

3 Prep
Gently combine the ingredients.

4 Presentation
Divide the compote into ½ cup servings of compote and top each with ⅓ cup Coconut Lemon Whip. Suggested garnish includes shaved lemon, lemon rind and 2 drops YL lemon oil.

---

1   My choice is raw honey or pure Grade B maple syrup, since these sweeteners are natural and easily accessible.

Hemp Seed Zucchini Pizza Crust

Serves 6
Yields 1 thin crust for 6 slices of pizza

Scrap Bowl contents (1 cup Zucchini Reduction, ½ cup Zucchini Sage Bisque)
Pecans, 1 cup, soaked and dehydrated
Flaxseeds, 2 tablespoons, ground to equal 3 packed tablespoons flax flour
Hemp seeds, ¼ cup, not soaked

1 Run
Grind pecans in a food processor until the texture resembles meal. Add the remaining ingredients and mix until even throughout. Remove to a solid dehydrator sheet.

2 Ease
Spread the mixture in a circular shape to fill the sheet completely. Form a raised crust around the edge. Score the crust into 6 pizza slices. Dehydrate at 105°F for 2 to 4 hours. Flip onto the mesh-lined tray and continue to dehydrate for 1 hour. Then flip the crust back to the original the position on the mesh-lined tray to avoid inverted pizza. Continue until dry, for approximately 6 to 8 hours.

3 Presentation
Store crust between two dehydrator trays wrapped in plastic wrap to secure and protect the crust for Day 6 dinner ('Roasted' Tomato Broccoli Pizza).

Day 6

Day 6 Outlook

Production	Grand Reduction
Breakfast	Beet Oregano Detox
Lunch	Beet Rosemary Borscht
Snack	Fuji Spearmint Smoothie + Fuji Spearmint Candy
Scrap recipe	Stuffed Basil Mushrooms and Beetballs
Dinner	'Roasted' Tomato Broccoli Pizza
Dessert	Banana Lemon Meringue Pie

Note: Some of today's recipes require certain ingredients to have been processed or prepared ahead of time. Plan accordingly if you are not following the book from beginning to end.

To prepare for today

1 Soak ½ cup (2 ounces) of packed, dry Irish moss in the refrigerator for dessert (Banana Lemon Meringue Pie) for 12-24 hours. Note: Irish moss doubles in weight and size when soaked. When measuring for ingredients, be mindful of whether the recipe calls for dry or soaked ingredients.

2 Designate a bowl for the leftover ingredients needed for the scrap recipe (Stuffed Basil Mushrooms and Beetballs).

Grand Reduction

Production

Yield varies by bowl

Cremini mushrooms, 2 pints (16 ounces), stems removed and reserved
Baby spinach, 1 package (5 ounces)
Broccoli florets ,1 head (no stems)
Grape tomatoes, 2 pints
Yellow onion, 1 small, roughly chopped
Beet, 1 medium, peeled and chopped
Cold pressed olive oil, 1¼ cup
Garlic, 1 bulb, pressed
Nama Shoyu, wheat-free Tamari or raw coconut aminos, ¼ cup
Himalayan salt, 1 teaspoon

1 Prep

To organize today's advanced reduction, begin by labeling five bowls: soup, stuffing, mushrooms, broccoli and pizza. Brush mushroom tops clean. Shred the stems by hand to resemble chicken and place into the broccoli bowl. Place 18 larger mushrooms in the mushrooms bowl and set aside. Slice the spinach with a chef knife and divide equally into the soup, stuffing and pizza bowls.

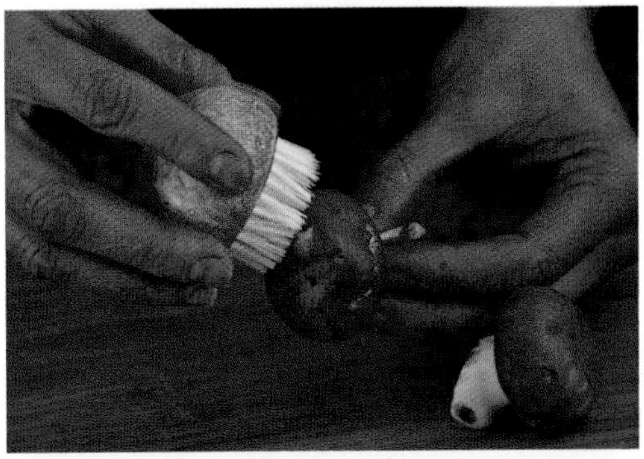

2 Run

Separately process the remaining mushrooms, broccoli, tomatoes, beet and onion through a food processor with the slice blade. Divide the sliced ingredients in the respective bowls as follows:

Soup (mushrooms, ⅓ of tomatoes, ½ of onion and beet, ⅕ olive oil, ⅕ of garlic, ¼ salt)

Stuffing (⅓ of tomatoes and ½ of onion, ⅕ olive oil, ⅕ of garlic, ¼ salt)

Mushrooms (whole mushrooms, ¼ cup Nama Shoyu, ⅕ olive oil, ⅕ of garlic)

Broccoli (broccoli, shredded mushroom stems, ⅕ olive oil, ⅕ of garlic, ¼ salt)

Pizza (⅓ of tomatoes and ⅓ of spinach, ⅕ olive oil, ⅕ of garlic, ¼ salt)

Divide the olive oil and garlic between all five bowls. Add the Nama Shoyu to the whole mushrooms. Divide the salt between four bowls, excluding the whole mushrooms bowl.

3 Ease

Evenly distribute the soup mix onto 2 solid dehydrator sheets. Evenly distribute the stuffing mix onto 1 solid dehydrator sheet. Dehydrate at 105°F for 3 hours. Turn trays halfway for balanced reduction. Label and refrigerate remaining bowls until needed in recipes.

After dehydrating, label and refrigerate the soup reduction for lunch (Beet Rosemary Borscht) and add the stuffing reduction to the scrap bowl for scrap recipe (Stuffed Basil Mushrooms and Beetballs).

Beet Oregano Detox

Serves 6
Yields 10 cups, 8 ounces per serving, plus 2 cups juice for Fuji Spearmint Smoothie and 2 cups for Beet Rosemary Borscht.

Beets, 8 medium, peeled and chopped
Carrots, 8 medium, peeled and chopped
Parsley, 1 bunch
Lemons, 4 quartered with rind
Celery, 2 bunches
Apples, 1 3-pound bag Fuji or 9 medium, roughly chopped
YL oregano essential oil, 1 drop
YL black pepper essential oil

1 Run

To organize today's 2-in-1 juice recipe, begin by labeling two pitchers: beet carrot parsley juice (which will become the Beet Oregano Detox) and lemon celery apple juice (which 2 cups will be refrigerated for the smoothie recipe and the remaining will be added to the beet carrot parsley juice). Extract the beets, carrots and parsley through a juicer. Set aside this juice in the corresponding pitcher and set aside the pulp for the scrap recipe. Without cleaning the juicer, extract the lemon, celery and apples. Set aside only 2 cups of this juice in the corresponding pitcher. Add the remaining lemon celery apple juice to the beet carrot parsley juice to make beet detox juice. Strain the juice for a smoother consistency, if desired. Stir to mix.

2 Ease

Label and refrigerate 2 cups lemon celery apple juice for the smoothie recipe (Fuji Spearmint Smoothie), ½ cup of the pulp to the scrap bowl for the scrap recipe (Stuffed Basil Mushrooms) and 2 cups of the beet detox juice for lunch (Beet Rosemary Borscht).

3 Presentation

Add oregano essential oil to the beet detox batch. Stir to mix. Divide juice into six servings. Add one drop of black pepper essential oil to each glass and stir when ready to serve.

Beet Rosemary Borscht

Serves 6

Red Dill Cabbage
Yields 1½ cups, ¼ cup per serving

Red cabbage, 1½ cups, finely shredded
YL dill essential oil, 1 drop
Himalayan salt, ½ teaspoon

1 Prep
Combine all of the ingredients and let set to wilt while preparing the soup.

Beet Rosemary Borscht
Yields 6 cups: 1 cup per serving

Soup Reduction, 2 packed cups reserved
Beet detox juice, 2 cups reserved
Brazil Nut Milk, 1 cup
Paprika, 1 tablespoon
Himalayan salt, ½ teaspoon
YL rosemary essential oil, 2 drops
YL black pepper essential oil, 1 drop
Cashew Mayonnaise, ⅓ cup reserved

2 Run
Blend ingredients in a high-speed blender until smooth.

3 Presentation
Divide borscht into 6 servings. Distribute ¼ cup Red Dill Cabbage to each bowl. Top each serving with 1 tablespoon of Cashew Mayonnaise, if desired. Suggested garnish includes diced cucumber, tomato, avocado, drizzles of olive oil, rosemary leaves and dashes of fresh ground pepper.

Fuji Spearmint Smoothie

Serves 6
Yields 7 cups smoothie: 8 ounces per serving, plus 1 cup reserved for candy

Lemon celery apple juice, 2 cups reserved
Brazil Nut Milk, 1 cup reserved
Bananas, 3 frozen
Pineapple, ½ 16-ounce package frozen
YL Power Meal protein powder, 2 scoops
YL spearmint essential oil

1 Run
Blend all of the ingredients, except the essential oil. Reserve 1 cup in the blender for the candy recipe (Fuji Spearmint Candy).

2 Presentations
Divide the smoothie into 6 servings. Add 1 drop spearmint essential oil to each glass and stir when ready to serve.

Fuji Spearmint Candy

Serves 6
Yields 2 cups: 4 trays or 36 pieces

Fuji Spearmint Smoothie, 1 cup reserved
Pineapple, ½ 16-ounce package frozen
Banana, 1 frozen
YL spearmint essential oil, 1 drop

3 Run
Blend all of the ingredients in a high-speed blender.

4 Ease
Spoon 9 tablespoons of the candy mixture per tray onto 4 solid dehydrator sheets. Dehydrate at 105°F until disks peel. This will occur from approximately 12 to 24 hours.

5 Presentation
Form the candy into creative shapes.

Stuffed Basil Mushrooms and Beetballs

Serves 6
Yields 1½ cups stuffing for 18 stuffed mushrooms and
12 beetballs

Scrap Bowl contents (Stuffing Reduction, ½ cup Beet
Oregano Detox pulp)
YL basil essential oil, 2 drops
Leftover marinade from mushrooms
Whole Mushrooms, 18 marinated

1 Prep
Process the scrap bowl contents, basil oil and
mushroom marinade in a food processor until the
texture resembles pate. Remove to a mixing bowl.

2 Ease
Arrange the marinated whole mushrooms on a solid
dehydrator sheet. Fill each cavity with ½ tablespoon
of the pate. To prepare the beetballs, roll 1 tablespoon
of the remaining pate into a ball and place on a solid
dehydrator sheet. Dehydrate at 105°F for 2 to 4 hours.

Recommendation: Since this is our last day of the food
feast and the next day is juicing, the scrap recipe
has been rearranged to serve before dinner as an
appetizer. The beetballs can be frozen and rewarmed
in the dehydrator for another raw week to be served
with Day 1 dinner (Yellow Squash Fennel Pasta).

'Roasted' Tomato Broccoli Pizza

Serves 6

Spinach Tomato Basil and Garlic Broccoli Thyme - Toppings
Yields 1 cup per topping

Pizza Marinade for Spinach Tomato Basil Topping, 1 cup reserved
YL basil essential oil, 1 drop

Garlic Broccoli Marinade for Garlic Broccoli Thyme Topping, 1 cup reserved
YL thyme essential oil, 1 drop

1 Ease
Separately and evenly distribute the marinades onto solid sheets and dehydrate at 105°F for 1 hour. Place the reductions in separate mixing bowls. Add the corresponding essential oils and toss well until coated throughout. Set aside until ready to assemble the pizza.

Brazil Nutmeg Mozzarella - Topping
Yields 1 cup

Brazil Nut Cheese, 1 cup
Lemon juice, ½ teaspoon fresh squeezed
Onion powder, ½ teaspoon
Nutmeg, ¼ teaspoon
Himalayan salt, ¾ teaspoon
White pepper, ⅛ teaspoon
YL nutmeg essential oil, 1 drop

2 Run
Combine all of the ingredients in a mixing bowl until well mixed. Set aside until ready to assemble the pizza.

'Roasted' Tomato Broccoli Pizza
Serves 6, 1 large slice per person

Brazil Nutmeg Mozzarella
Garlic Broccoli Thyme
Spinach Tomato Basil
6 slices reserved Hemp Seed Pizza Crust

3 Presentation
To assemble pizza, spread 6 slices of the Hemp Seed Pizza Crust with the Brazil Nutmeg Mozzarella. Top each slice with Garlic Broccoli Thyme and Spinach Tomato Basil. Suggested garnish includes sliced tomatoes, basil, olives and any left-over components from previous days, such as Cashew Mayonnaise and the Eggplant Sausage.

Banana Lemon Meringue Pie

Serves 6

Butter Lemon Crust

Yields 2½ cups to fill a 7-inch springform pan, plus 1 cup reserved

Almonds, 2 cups, soaked and dehydrated
Pine nuts, ½ cup
Himalayan salt, ½ teaspoon
YL lemon essential oil, 4 drops

1 Run
Grind the almonds in a food processor until fine. Add the pine nuts and continue until mixed throughout. Add the salt and lemon essential oil and process it until the mix sticks together. Remove and add 1 cup of the crust to the Day 6 scrap bowl for scrap recipe (Stuffed Basil Mushrooms).

Banana Lemon Meringue Pie Filling

Yields 4 cups pie filling

Irish moss, 4 ounces, soaked (equals dry packed ½ cup or 2 ounces)
Young coconut water, 1 cup (approximately 1 coconut)
Bananas, 3 frozen
Sweetener of choice[1], ¾ cup
YL lemon essential oil, 10 drops
Turmeric powder, ¾ teaspoon
Himalayan salt, ¼ teaspoon
Coconut Lemon Whip, 4 cups reserved

3 Prep
Gently rinse Irish Moss in very cold water until the debris is removed. Do not over rinse or moss will loose its gelatinous attribute.

2 Ease
Press the mixture into the bottom of a round 7-inch springform pan. Set it aside to make the pie filling.

4 Run
Blend moss in a high-speed blender with coconut water until smooth. Add the frozen bananas (to keep mixture cool), sweetener, lemon oil, turmeric powder, salt and blend well. Mixture can be warm, but not hot or moss will loose its gelatinous attribute.

5 Ease
Pour the filling into a springform pan. Cover with plastic wrap and freeze until set.

6 Presentation
When ready to eat, remove the pie from the freezer and fill with the refrigerated Coconut Lemon Whip for meringue. Slice it into 6 pieces and rest to allow the filling to completely thaw. Suggested garnish includes a lemon wedge, sliced bananas and 2 drops of YL lemon oil per serving. See page 100.

---

1   My choice is raw honey or pure Grade B maple syrup, since these sweeteners are natural and easily accessible.

Day 7

Day 7 Juice Feast Outlook

Before Breakfast	Fizz Fusion, AM BM Sweep, Inner Defense™
Breakfast	8V Black Pepper Cocktail
Mid-Morning Snack	Citrus Ginger Splash
Early Lunch	Carrot Orange Milk
Late Lunch	Cucumber Dill Tonic
Afternoon Snack	Lavender Ginger Lemonade
Dinner	Beet Oregano Detox
Before Bedtime	Fizz Fusion, PM BM Sweep, Life 5™

Note: The following juices are the same as introduced in the breakfast recipes of the Raw Food Feast. The yields and instructions for the juices have changed to serve two. Increase the quantity for more servings. The Young Living (YL) products included in this juice feast are recommended for a more complete detox, but not required. When juicing for consecutive days, increase the quantity and store extra juice for the following day(s). It is recommended to seal the juice in glass jars by using a vacuum sealing system with a jar attachment to maintain freshness. Refrigerate up to 48 hours or fill a glass jar to the top with juice and cap it with the lid to reduce exposure to air. Refrigerate up to 24 hours.

Before Breakfast

1 Fizz Fusion ~ upon waking
Serves 1

YL Alkalime*, 1 teaspoon
Distilled water[1], 8 ounces

2 AM BM Sweep ~ early morning
Serves 1

Lemon, 1 medium, juiced
Lime, 1 medium, juiced
Warm filtered water, 6 ounces
YL ICP*, 2 teaspoons

3 Inner Defense* - Take 1 capsule

Juice Feast - Breakfast through Dinner
See the following pages for juice recipes.

---

1   Distilled water is necessary with this product as the minerals in Alkalime are precisely balanced for the greatest absorption and effectiveness.

Before Bedtime

1 Fizz Fusion ~ Bedtime (same recipe as morning)
Serves 1

2 PM BM Sweep ~ Bedtime (same recipe as morning)
Serves 1

3 Life 5 Probiotic* - Take 1 capsule at least 8 hours after taking Inner Defense.

Note: Melon may be eaten throughout the day when in season to help with the craving to chew. Eat separately 15 minutes before and after drinking to ensure stomach is empty. In addition, a smoothie (particularly a green smoothie) can be added as a dessert if needed.

*Optional YL Products added to enhance and speed detox:

Alkalime ~ This specially designed alkaline mineral powder from Young Living Essential Oils contains an array of high-alkaline salts and other yeast and fungus fighting elements, such as citric acid and essential oils. Its precisely balanced, acid-neutralizing mineral formulation helps preserve the body's proper pH balance – the cornerstone of health. By boosting blood alkalinity, yeast and fungus are deprived of the acidic terrain they require to flourish. The effectiveness of other essential oils is enhanced when the body's blood and tissues are alkaline.

ICP ~ ICP Multiple Fiber Beverage from Young Living Essential Oils is an unique source of fiber and bulk for the diet and helps speed the transit time of waste matter through the intestinal tract. Psyllium, oat bran, flax and rice bran are specifically balanced in ICP to eliminate allergy symptoms that many people experience when taking Psyllium alone. Essential oils enhance ICP's flavor and may help dispel gas and pain. This formula is unsurpassed as an aid in enhancing normal bowel function.

Inner Defense – Each liquid softgel contains a proprietary blend of essential oils rich in thymol, carvacrol and eugenol and dissolve quickly for maximum results. Inner Defense reinforces the body's systemic defenses and promotes healthy respiratory and immune function and immune, while creating an unfriendly terrain for yeast/fungus.

Life 5 ~ A blend from Young Living Essential Oils of the most resilient probiotics studied with proven ability to colonize the gut and promote immunity, infection-resistance, and vitamin synthesis. Includes two new super-strains that have the best adhesion to any probiotic known: Acidophilus ramnosus HN001 and Bifidobacterium lactis HN019. It also contains super-strains of B. bifidus, L. acidophilus, and S. thermophilus. A special prebiotic mix was developed especially for these blends, consisting of proprietary complex of calcium, lactoferrin and other synergistics to provide unmatched enhancement of culture growth and implantation inside the body.

8V Black Pepper Cocktail

Serves 2
Yields 1 pint

Baby spinach, 2 cups (2 ounces)
Cherry tomatoes, 1 pint
Carrots, 2 medium, peeled
Cucumber, ½ medium, sliced lengthwise
Red bell pepper, ½ medium, roughly chopped
Beet, ¼ medium, peeled and roughly chopped
Parsley, ½ cup
Celery, 2 medium stalks
YL black pepper essential oil

1 Run
Extract the produce through a juicer. Strain the juice for a smoother consistency, if desired. Stir to mix.

2 Ease
Seal, label and refrigerate extra juice for consecutive days, if desired.

3 Presentation
Add 1 drop of black pepper oil to each glass and stir when ready to serve.

Citrus Ginger Splash

Serves 2
Yields 1 pint

Valencia oranges, 3 medium, halved
Grapefruit, 1 medium, halved
Lemon, 1 medium, halved
Lime, 1 large, halved
YL ginger, lemon, orange and grapefruit essential oils

1 Run
Use a citrus juicer to juice the fruit. Strain the juice for a smoother consistency, if desired. Stir to mix.

2 Ease
Seal, label and refrigerate extra juice for consecutive days, if desired.

3 Presentation
Add 2 drops of each essential oil to each glass and stir when ready to serve.

Carrot Orange Milk

Serves 2
Yields 1 pint

Carrots, 1 bag (2 pounds or 13 carrots), peeled
YL orange oil

1 Run
Extract the carrots through a juicer. Strain the juice for a smoother consistency, if desired. Stir to mix.

2 Ease
Seal, label and refrigerate extra juice for consecutive days, if desired.

3 Presentation
Add 2 drops of orange oil to each glass and stir when ready to serve.

Cucumber Dill Tonic

Serves 2
Yields 1 pint

Cucumber, 1 large
Green apple, 1 medium, sliced
Rainbow chard, 2 large leaves
Lacinato kale, 3 large leaves
Romaine lettuce, 6 large leaves
Celery, 4 stalks
YL dill essential oil

1 Run
Extract the produce through a juicer. Strain the juice for a smoother consistency, if desired. Stir to mix.

2 Ease
Seal, label and refrigerate extra juice for consecutive days, if desired.

3 Presentation
Add 1 drop of dill essential oil to each glass and stir when ready to serve.

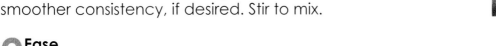

Lavender Ginger Lemonade

Serves 2
Yields 1 pint

Purple or red grapes, 1 pound
Green and/or Fuji apples, 3 medium
Celery, 2 medium stalks
Lemon, 1 medium, quartered with rind
Ginger, 1 small slice
YL lavender essential oil, 1 drop or less
YL lemon essential oil
YL ginger essential oil

1 Run
Extract the produce through a juicer. Strain the juice for a smoother consistency, if desired. Stir to mix.

2 Ease
Seal, label and refrigerate extra juice for consecutive days, if desired.

3 Presentation
Add lavender oil to the batch. Be careful not to add too much. Use a toothpick to dip into the bottle if less than a drop is desired. Stir to mix. Divide juice into two servings. Add 2 drops each of lemon and ginger oil to each glass and stir when ready to serve.

Optional: This juice can be made without grapes if organic cannot be found. Increase apples to 6 and use 3 green and 3 Fuji apples.

Recommended: This juice can be diluted with filtered water or organic green tea, served over crushed ice and sipped throughout the day.

Beet Oregano Detox

Serves 2
Yields 1 pint

Beets, 3 medium, peeled and chopped
Carrots, 3 medium, peeled and chopped
Celery, 3 stalks
Apples, 1 medium Fuji, roughly chopped
Lemon, 1 quartered with rind
Parsley, ½ bunch
YL oregano essential oil, 1 drop or less
YL black pepper essential oil

1 Run
Extract the produce through a juicer. Strain the juice for a smoother consistency, if desired. Stir to mix.

2 Ease
Seal, label and refrigerate extra juice for consecutive days, if desired.

3 Presentation
Add oregano oil to the batch. Be careful not to add too much. Use a toothpick to dip into the bottle if less than a drop is desired. Stir to mix. Divide juice into two servings. Add 1 drop of black pepper oil to each glass and stir when ready to serve.

Shopping Lists

Base Recipe Shopping List

Fruits
- [ ] Bananas – 29 regular
- [ ] Lemons – 2 medium

Nuts and seeds
- [ ] Almonds – 5 cups (26 ounces)
- [ ] Brazil nuts – 3 cups (16 ounces)
- [ ] Cashews – 4 cups (20 ounces)
- [ ] Pecans – 4 cups (14 ounces)
- [ ] Walnuts 1 cup (4 ounces)

Spices/Seasonings
- [ ] Mustard, ground – ½ teaspoons
- [ ] Salt, Himalayan – 1 ½ teaspoons

Condiments
- [ ] Apple cider vinegar, raw – 1 tablespoon
- [ ] Solaray Multidophilus Powder – 1 teaspoon

Sweetener
- [ ] Choice of sweetener[1] – 1 teaspoon

---

1   Choose a healthy sweetener from a local health food store or a reputable company on the Internet. My choice is raw honey and pure Grade B maple syrup, since these sweeteners are natural and easily accessible.

Vegetables

- [ ] Beets – 1 medium
- [ ] Carrots – 4 medium
- [ ] Celery – 8 medium
- [ ] Cucumbers – 2 medium
- [ ] Onion, yellow – ½ medium
- [ ] Peppers, red bell – 8 medium
- [ ] Spinach, baby – 1 package
- [ ] Squash, yellow – 6 medium
- [ ] Tomatoes, cherry – 3 pints
- [ ] Tomatoes, Roma – 12 medium

Fruits

- [ ] Avocados – 6 medium
- [ ] Bananas – 4 medium (not including 5 frozen bananas from the Base Recipe Shopping List)
- [ ] Dates, Medjool – 1 plump
- [ ] Kiwifruit – 6 regular
- [ ] Limes – 8 large

Fresh herbs

- [ ] Garlic – 6 medium cloves
- [ ] Parsley – 1 bunch

Nuts and seeds

- [ ] Flaxseeds – ½ cup seeds or ⅔ cup ground flour

Frozen fruit

- [ ] Cherries – 1 10-ounce package
- [ ] Raspberries – 1 12-ounce package

Fats

- [ ] Olive oil, first cold pressing – ½ cup, plus 3 tablespoons

Spices/Seasonings

- [ ] Italian Seasoning – 1 tablespoon
- [ ] Salt, Himalayan – 3 tablespoons, plus 1 ½ teaspoons

Condiments

- [ ] Tomatoes, sundried in oil – ½ 8.5-ounce jar (½ saved for Day 5)

Young Living essential oils

- [ ] Basil oil – 2 drops
- [ ] Black pepper oil – 6 drops
- [ ] Clove oil – 2 drops
- [ ] Cinnamon bark oil – 3 drops
- [ ] Fennel oil – 2 drops
- [ ] Marjoram oil – 1 drop
- [ ] Peppermint oil – 1 drop

Sweetener

- [ ] Choice of sweetener[1] - 1 cup, plus 2 tablespoons

Young Living products

- [ ] Power Meal Protein Powder – 2 scoops or 1.8 ounces

Garnish ingredients

- [ ] Avocados – 2 medium
- [ ] Basil, fresh leaves – 6 sprigs
- [ ] Cucumbers – 1 medium
- [ ] Italian seasoning – 1 tablespoon
- [ ] Marjoram – 6 sprigs
- [ ] Olive oil, first cold pressing – 2 tablespoons
- [ ] Tomatoes – 2 medium

---

1   My choice is raw honey or Grade B maple syrup, since these sweeteners are natural and easily accessible.

Day 2 Shopping List

Vegetables
- [ ] Carrots – 5 medium
- [ ] Cauliflower – 1 medium head
- [ ] Onion, yellow – ½ medium
- [ ] Peppers, red bell – 6 medium
- [ ] Sprouts of choice – 1 pint

Fruits
- [ ] Avocados – 2 medium
- [ ] Bananas – None needed if you already have 4 frozen bananas from the Base Recipe Shopping List
- [ ] Coconuts, young – 5 (or 4 ½ cups coconut water and 2 cups packed meat)
- [ ] Grapefruit – 4 medium
- [ ] Lemons – 2 medium
- [ ] Limes – 2 large
- [ ] Oranges, Valencia – 12 medium

Fresh herbs
- [ ] Garlic – 6 medium cloves
- [ ] Ginger – 2 grated tablespoons or 3 ounces

Nuts and seeds
- [ ] Macadamia – 1 cup or 6 ounces
- [ ] Pine nuts – ⅓ cup
- [ ] Sesame seeds, raw hulled – 2 tablespoons
- [ ] Sunflower seeds, raw hulled – 1 cup

Dried fruit
- [ ] Coconut, dried flakes – 2 cups

Frozen fruit
- [ ] Strawberries – 1 12-ounce package

Sea vegetables
- [ ] Nori sheets – 10 dried sheets, not roasted

Fats
- [ ] Coconut oil, raw virgin – ½ cup
- [ ] Sesame oil, raw – ½ cup
- [ ] Sesame oil, toasted – ¼ cup

Spices/Seasonings
- [ ] Five-spice powder – 1 teaspoon
- [ ] Salt, Himalayan – 1 teaspoon

Condiments
- [ ] Miso, chickpea – 1 tablespoon
- [ ] Nama Shoyu, wheat-free Tamari or raw coconut aminos – ½ cup, plus 2 tablespoons
- [ ] Red curry paste, Thai Kitchen – 2 tablespoons

Sweetener
- [ ] Choice of sweetener[1] - 3 tablespoons

Young Living essential oils
- [ ] Black pepper oil - 4 drops
- [ ] Ginger oil – 18 drops
- [ ] Grapefruit oil – 32 drops
- [ ] Lemon oil – 12 drops
- [ ] Lemongrass oil – 2 drops
- [ ] Orange oil – 12 drops

Young Living products
- [ ] Power Meal Protein Powder – 2 scoops or 1.8 ounces

Garnish ingredients
- [ ] Basil, Thai – 2 tablespoons minced
- [ ] Cabbage, Napa – 1 cup shredded
- [ ] Onions, green scallion – 4 medium
- [ ] Sesame oil, toasted – 2 tablespoons

Reserved recipe
- [ ] Reserved Key Lime Mousse from Day 1

---

1   My choice is raw honey or Grade B maple syrup, since these sweeteners are natural and easily accessible.

Vegetables
- [ ] Carrots – 1 10-pound bag, plus 1 2-pound bag or 13 medium
- [ ] Celery – 4 medium stalks
- [ ] Lettuce, Romaine – 12 medium hearts
- [ ] Onion, yellow – ½ medium

Fruits
- [ ] Avocado – 1 medium
- [ ] Bananas – 3 medium (not including 4 frozen bananas from the Base Recipe Shopping List)
- [ ] Coconuts, young – 4 (or 2 cups packed meat)
- [ ] Dates, Medjool – 12 plump
- [ ] Oranges, Valencia – 12 medium
- [ ] Pears – 7 medium

Fresh herbs
- [ ] Garlic – 2 medium cloves
- [ ] Ginger – 1 grated tablespoon

Nuts and seeds
- [ ] Flaxseeds – ½ cup or ⅔ cup ground flour
- [ ] Pecans – 1 cup or 4 ounces
- [ ] Pine nuts – ¼ cup

Fats
- [ ] Coconut oil, raw virgin – 3 tablespoons
- [ ] Grapeseed oil – ½ cup
- [ ] Olive oil, first cold pressing – 3 tablespoons

Spices/Seasonings
- [ ] Cinnamon, ground – 2 teaspoons
- [ ] Cumin, ground – 1 tablespoon
- [ ] Salt, Himalayan– 1 tablespoon, plus ¾ teaspoon

Flavoring (alcohol-free)[1]
- [ ] Vanilla – 1 teaspoon

Condiments
- [ ] Apple cider vinegar, raw – 1 tablespoon
- [ ] Capers – 1 3.5-ounce jar

Sweetener
- [ ] Choice of sweetener[2] - ¼ cup

Young Living essential oils
- [ ] Cinnamon bark oil – 4 drops
- [ ] Coriander oil – 1 drop
- [ ] Dill oil – 3 drops
- [ ] Lemon oil – 4 drops
- [ ] Nutmeg oil – 2 drops
- [ ] Orange oil – 12 drops

Young Living products
- [ ] Power Meal Protein Powder – 2 scoops or 1.8 ounces

Garnish ingredients
- [ ] Bananas – 2 regular
- [ ] Cucumber – 1 medium
- [ ] Cumin, ground – 1 tablespoon
- [ ] Cinnamon, ground – 1 tablespoon
- [ ] Dill, fresh – 2 minced tablespoons
- [ ] Olive oil, first cold pressing – 2 teaspoons
- [ ] Tomato – 2 medium

---

1   Instead of imitation or alcohol-filled extracts, choose alcohol-free flavorings.

2   My choice is raw honey or Grade B maple syrup, since these sweeteners are natural and easily accessible.

Day 4 Shopping List

Vegetables
- [ ] Celery – 1 bunch, plus 3 medium stalks
- [ ] Chard, rainbow – 1 head
- [ ] Cucumbers – 13 medium
- [ ] Kale, Lacinato – 1 head
- [ ] Lettuce, Romaine – 1 head
- [ ] Onion, red – ¼ medium

Fruits
- [ ] Apples, green – 4 medium
- [ ] Bananas – 3 medium (not including 4 frozen bananas from the Base Recipe Shopping List)
- [ ] Oranges, navel – 6 medium
- [ ] Tangerines – 9 large or 2 ½ cup fresh juice

Nuts and seeds
- [ ] Cashews – 1 cup or 5 ounces
- [ ] Flaxseeds – 2 tablespoons or 3 packed Tablespoons of flour
- [ ] Hemp seeds – ¼ cup
- [ ] Sunflower seeds – 1 cup or 5 ounces

Sea vegetables
- [ ] Dulse, whole – ¼ cup minced

Dried fruit
- [ ] Cranberries, juice-sweetened – 1 cup

Frozen fruit
- [ ] Pineapple – 1 16-ounce package

Fats
- [ ] Coconut oil, raw virgin or cacao butter, raw – ½ cup
- [ ] Grapeseed oil – ½ cup

Spices/Seasonings
- [ ] Salt, Himalayan – 1 tablespoon, plus 1 teaspoon

Super foods
- [ ] Cacao Powder, raw or carob powder, roasted – 1 cup

Condiments
- [ ] Apple cider vinegar, raw – 2 tablespoons
- [ ] Nama Shoyu, wheat-free Tamari or raw coconut aminos – ½ teaspoon

Sweetener
- [ ] Choice of sweetener[1] – 3 tablespoons
- [ ] Grade B maple syrup – ¾ cup

Young Living essential oils
- [ ] Cinnamon bark oil – 1 drop
- [ ] Dill oil – 6 drops
- [ ] Lemon oil – 2 drops
- [ ] Orange oil – 20 drops
- [ ] Tangerine oil – 8 drops
- [ ] Tarragon oil – 1 drop

Young Living products
- [ ] Power Meal Protein Powder – 2 scoops or 1.8 ounces

Garnish ingredients
- [ ] Avocados – 2 medium
- [ ] Cucumber – 1 medium
- [ ] Cinnamon, ground – 1 tablespoon
- [ ] Olive oil, first cold pressing – 2 tablespoons
- [ ] Orange oil – 18 drops
- [ ] Pepper, ground – 1 tablespoon
- [ ] Salad, fresh baby herb – 1 5-ounce package
- [ ] Spirulina – 1 tablespoon
- [ ] Tomato – 7 medium

Reserved recipe
- [ ] Reserved Caramel Orange Cream from Day 3

1   My choice is raw honey or Grade B maple syrup, since these sweeteners are natural and easily accessible.

Vegetables

- ☐ Celery – 8 medium stalks
- ☐ Eggplant – 2 medium
- ☐ Onion, yellow – 1 small
- ☐ Squash, zucchini – 16 medium

Fruits

- ☐ Apples, Fuji – 4 medium
- ☐ Apples, green – 4 medium
- ☐ Bananas – 4 medium (not including 5 frozen bananas from the Base Recipe Shopping List)
- ☐ Coconuts, young – 8 (or 4 cups packed meat, 1 cup reserved water for day 6 dessert)
- ☐ Grapes, purple or red – 3 pounds
- ☐ Lemons – 8 medium

Fresh herbs

- ☐ Garlic – 9 medium cloves
- ☐ Ginger – 1 inch (1 ounce) with peel
- ☐ Sage – 1 teaspoon minced

Nuts and seeds

- ☐ Flaxseeds – 2 tablespoons or 3 tablespoons packed flour
- ☐ Hemp seeds – ¼ cup
- ☐ Pine nuts – 2 cups (11 ounces)

Sea vegetables

- ☐ Dulse – 1 tablespoon packed

Frozen fruit

- ☐ Blueberries – 2 8-ounce packages

Fats

- ☐ Coconut oil, raw virgin – ⅓ cup
- ☐ Olive oil, first cold pressing – ¾ cup
- ☐ White truffle oil – 1 tablespoons

Spices/Seasonings

- ☐ Anise, whole seed – 2 teaspoons
- ☐ Onion, dried flakes – 1 tablespoon
- ☐ Salt, Himalayan – 2 tablespoons, plus 2 teaspoons

Flavoring (alcohol-free)

- ☐ Almond – 2 tablespoons

Condiments

- ☐ Apple cider vinegar, raw – 1 teaspoon
- ☐ Nama Shoyu, wheat-free Tamari or raw coconut aminos – 1 tablespoon
- ☐ Tomatoes, sundried in oil – ½ 8.5-ounce jar (½ reserved from day 1)

Sweetener

- ☐ Choice of sweetener[1] – ⅔ cup

Young Living essential oils

- ☐ Fennel oil – 2 drops
- ☐ Ginger oil – 12 drops
- ☐ Lavender oil – 2 drops
- ☐ Lemon oil – 37 drops
- ☐ Sage oil – 1 drop

Young Living products

- ☐ Power Meal Protein Powder – 2 scoops or 1.8 ounces

Garnish ingredients

- ☐ Celery – 2 medium stalks
- ☐ Fennel, fresh leaves – 2 sprigs
- ☐ Green Tea – 1 box to dilute breakfast juice
- ☐ Lemon – 1 medium
- ☐ Lemon essential oil – 12 drops
- ☐ Olive oil, first cold pressing – 2 tablespoons
- ☐ Onion, purple – ½ medium
- ☐ Pepper, ground – 1 tablespoon
- ☐ Sage, whole – 2 tablespoons minced
- ☐ Tomato – 2 medium

---

1   My choice is raw honey or Grade B maple syrup, since these sweeteners are natural and easily accessible.

Day 6 Shopping List

Vegetables
☐ Beets – 9 medium
☐ Broccoli – 1 head
☐ Cabbage, red – 1 ½ shredded cups
☐ Carrots – 8 medium
☐ Celery – 2 bunches
☐ Mushrooms, Cremini – 2 pints (16 ounces)
☐ Onion, yellow – 1 small
☐ Spinach, baby – 1 5-ounce package
☐ Tomatoes, grape or cherry – 2 pints

Fruits
☐ Apples, Fuji – 1 3-pound bag or 9 medium
☐ Bananas – None needed if you already have 7 frozen bananas from the Base Recipe Shopping List
☐ Lemons – 5 medium

Fresh herbs
☐ Garlic – 1 bulb
☐ Parsley – I bunch

Nuts and seeds
☐ Pine nuts – ½ cup

Sea vegetables
☐ Irish Moss, dry – ½ cup packed

Frozen fruit
☐ Pineapple – 1 16-ounce package

Fats
☐ Olive oil, first cold pressing – 1 ¼ cup

Spices/Seasonings
☐ Nutmeg – ¼ teaspoon
☐ Onion, powder – ½ teaspoon
☐ Paprika – 1 tablespoon
☐ Pepper, white – ⅛ teaspoon
☐ Salt, Himalayan – 1 tablespoon
☐ Turmeric powder – ¾ teaspoon

Condiments
☐ Nama Shoyu, wheat-free Tamari or raw coconut aminos – ¼ cup

Sweetener
☐ Choice of sweetener[1] – ¾ cup, plus 2 tablespoons

Young Living essential oils
☐ Basil oil – 3 drops
☐ Black pepper oil – 7 drops
☐ Dill oil – 1 drop
☐ Lemon oil – 14 drops
☐ Nutmeg oil – 1 drop
☐ Oregano oil – 1 drop
☐ Rosemary oil – 2 drops
☐ Spearmint oil – 7 drops
☐ Thyme oil – 1 drop

Young Living products
☐ Power Meal Protein Powder – 2 scoops or 1.8 ounces

Garnish ingredients
☐ Avocado – 2 medium
☐ Basil leaves – ¼ cup packed
☐ Cucumber – 1 medium
☐ Olives, pitted - 1 jar
☐ Olive oil, first cold pressing – 2 tablespoons
☐ Pepper, ground– 1 tablespoon
☐ Tomato – 2 medium

Reserved recipe
☐ Reserved Coconut Lemon Whip from Day 3

---

1   My choice is raw honey or Grade B maple syrup, since these sweeteners are natural and easily accessible.

Vegetables

☐ Beets – 3 medium, plus ¼ medium
☐ Carrots – 1 bag (2 pounds or 13 carrots), plus 5 medium
☐ Celery – 11 stalks
☐ Chard, rainbow – 2 large leaves
☐ Cucumbers – 1 large, plus ½ medium
☐ Kale, Lacinato – 3 large leaves
☐ Lettuce, Romaine – 6 large leaves
☐ Peppers, red bell – ½ medium
☐ Spinach, baby – 2 cups (2 ounces)
☐ Tomatoes, cherry – 1 pint

Fruits

☐ Apples, Fuji – 1 medium
☐ Apples, green – 4 medium
☐ Grapefruit – 1 medium
☐ Grapes, purple or red – 1 pound
☐ Lemons – 5 medium
☐ Limes – 3 medium
☐ Oranges, Valencia – 3 medium

Fresh herbs

☐ Ginger – 1 small slice
☐ Parsley – ½ bunch, plus ½ cup

Young Living essential oils

☐ Black pepper oil – 4 drops
☐ Dill oil – 2 drops
☐ Ginger oil – 8 drops
☐ Grapefruit oil – 4 drops
☐ Lavender oil – 1 drop
☐ Lemon oil – 8 drops
☐ Orange oil – 8 drops
☐ Oregano oil – 1 drop

Vegetables

- [ ] Beets – 10 medium
- [ ] Broccoli – 1 head
- [ ] Cabbage, red – 1 ½ cups shredded
- [ ] Carrots – 1 10-pound bag and 1 2-pound bags, plus 17 medium
- [ ] Cauliflower – 1 medium head
- [ ] Celery – 3 bunches, plus 23 medium stalks
- [ ] Chard, rainbow – 1 head
- [ ] Cucumbers – 15 medium
- [ ] Eggplant – 2 medium
- [ ] Kale, Lacinato – 1 head
- [ ] Lettuce, Romaine – 12 medium hearts, 1 head
- [ ] Mushrooms, cremini – 2 pints (16 ounces)
- [ ] Onion, red – ¼ medium
- [ ] Onions, yellow – 1 ½ medium and 2 small
- [ ] Peppers, red bell – 14 medium
- [ ] Spinach, baby – 2 5-ounce packages
- [ ] Sprouts of choice – 1 pint
- [ ] Squash, yellow – 6 medium
- [ ] Squash, zucchini – 16 medium
- [ ] Tomatoes, cherry – 3 pints
- [ ] Tomatoes, grape - 2 pints
- [ ] Tomatoes, Roma – 12 medium

Fruits

- [ ] Apples, Fuji – 13 medium
- [ ] Apples, green – 8 medium
- [ ] Avocados – 9 medium
- [ ] Bananas – 43 medium
- [ ] Coconuts, young – 17 medium (or 5 ½ cups coconut water and 8 cups packed meat)
- [ ] Dates, Medjool – 13 plump
- [ ] Grapefruit – 4 medium
- [ ] Grapes, purple or red – 3 pounds
- [ ] Kiwifruit – 6 regular
- [ ] Lemons – 17 medium
- [ ] Limes – 10 large
- [ ] Oranges, navel- 6 medium
- [ ] Oranges, Valencia – 24 medium
- [ ] Pears – 7 medium
- [ ] Tangerines – 9 large (or 2 ½ cups juice)

Fresh herbs

- [ ] Garlic – 23 medium cloves, plus 1 bulb
- [ ] Ginger – 3 grated tablespoons, 1 inch (1 ounce)
- [ ] Parsley – 2 bunches
- [ ] Sage – 1 teaspoon minced

Nuts and seeds

- [ ] Almonds – 5 cups (26 ounces)
- [ ] Brazil nuts – 3 cups (16 ounces)
- [ ] Cashews – 5 cups (25 ounces)
- [ ] Flaxseed – 1 ¼ cup or 1 ½ cup ground packed flour
- [ ] Hemp seeds – ½ cup
- [ ] Macadamia – 1 cup (6 ounces)
- [ ] Pecans – 5 cups (18 ounces)
- [ ] Pine nuts – 3 cups and 2 tablespoons (18 ounces)
- [ ] Sesame seeds, raw hulled – 2 tablespoons
- [ ] Sunflower seeds, raw hulled – 2 cups (10 ounces)
- [ ] Walnuts – 1 cup (4 ounces)

Sea vegetables

- [ ] Dulse, whole – ¼ cup minced, plus 1 tablespoon packed
- [ ] Irish Moss, dry – ½ cup packed (2 ounces)
- [ ] Nori sheets – 10 untoasted dried sheets

Dried fruit

☐ Coconut, dried flakes – 2 cups
☐ Cranberries, juice-sweetened – 1 cup

Frozen fruit

☐ Blueberries – 2 8-ounce packages
☐ Cherries – 1 10-ounce package
☐ Pineapple – 2 16-ounce packages
☐ Raspberries – 1 12-ounce package
☐ Strawberries – 1 12-ounce package

Fats

☐ Coconut oil, raw virgin – 1 ½ cup, plus 3 tablespoons
☐ Grapeseed oil – 1 cup
☐ Olive oil, first cold pressing – 2 ⅔ cup
☐ Sesame oil, raw – ½ cup
☐ Sesame oil, toasted – ¼ cup
☐ White truffle oil – 1 tablespoons

Spices/Seasonings

☐ Anise, whole seed – 2 teaspoons
☐ Five-spice powder – 1 teaspoon
☐ Cinnamon, ground – 2 teaspoons
☐ Cumin, ground – 1 tablespoon
☐ Italian Seasoning – 1 tablespoon
☐ Mustard, ground – ½ teaspoon
☐ Nutmeg, – ¼ teaspoon
☐ Onion powder – ½ teaspoon
☐ Onion, dried flakes – 1 tablespoon
☐ Paprika – 1 tablespoon
☐ Pepper, white – ⅛ teaspoon
☐ Salt, Himalayan – ½ cup and 3 teaspoons
☐ Turmeric powder – ¾ teaspoon

Flavorings (alcohol-free)[1]

☐ Almond – 2 tablespoons
☐ Vanilla – 1 teaspoon

Condiments

☐ Apple cider vinegar, raw – ¼ cup, plus 1 teaspoon
☐ Capers – 1 3.5-ounce jar
☐ Miso, chickpea – 1 tablespoon
☐ Nama Shoyu, wheat-free Tamari or raw coconut aminos – 1 cup
☐ Red curry paste, Thai Kitchen – 2 tablespoons
☐ Solaray Multidophilus Powder – 1 teaspoon
☐ Sundried tomatoes in oil – 1 8.5-ounce jar

Sweetener

☐ Choice of sweetener[2] – 3 ¼ cup, plus 3 tablespoons
☐ Grade B maple syrup – ¾ cup

Super foods

☐ Cacao Powder, raw or carob powder, roasted – 1 cup

Young Living essential oils

☐ Basil oil – 5 drops
☐ Black pepper oil – 17 drops
☐ Cinnamon bark oil – 8 drops
☐ Clove oil – 2 drops
☐ Coriander oil – 1 drop
☐ Dill oil – 10 drops
☐ Fennel oil – 4 drops
☐ Ginger oil – 30 drops
☐ Grapefruit oil – 32 drops
☐ Lavender oil – 2 drops
☐ Lemon oil – 69 drops
☐ Lemongrass oil – 2 drops
☐ Marjoram oil – 1 drop
☐ Nutmeg oil – 3 drops
☐ Orange oil – 44 drops

---

1   Instead of imitation or alcohol-filled extracts, choose alcohol-free flavorings.

2   My choice is raw honey or Grade B maple syrup, since these sweeteners are natural and easily accessible.

Master Shopping List

- [ ] Oregano oil – 1 drop
- [ ] Peppermint oil – 1 drop
- [ ] Rosemary oil – 2 drops
- [ ] Sage oil – 1 drop
- [ ] Spearmint oil – 7 drops
- [ ] Tangerine oil – 8 drops
- [ ] Tarragon oil – 1 drop
- [ ] Thyme oil – 1 drop

Young Living products
- [ ] Power Meal Protein Powder – 12 scoops or 10.8 ounces

Garnish ingredients (optional)

Garnish - Vegetables
- [ ] Cabbage, Napa – 1 shredded cup
- [ ] Celery – 2 medium stalks
- [ ] Cucumbers – 4 medium
- [ ] Onion, purple – ½ whole
- [ ] Onions, green scallions – 4 medium
- [ ] Sage, whole – 2 tablespoons minced
- [ ] Salad, fresh baby herb – 1 5-ounce package
- [ ] Tomatoes – 15 medium

Garnish - Fruit
- [ ] Avocados – 6 medium
- [ ] Banana – 2 regular
- [ ] Lemon – 1 medium

Garnish - Fresh herbs
- [ ] Basil, fresh leaves – 6 sprigs, plus ¼ cup packed
- [ ] Basil, Thai – 2 minced tablespoons
- [ ] Cinnamon, ground – 2 tablespoons
- [ ] Cumin, ground – 1 tablespoon
- [ ] Dill, fresh – 2 minced tablespoons
- [ ] Fennel, fresh leaves - 2 sprigs
- [ ] Green tea – 1 box to dilute breakfast juice

- [ ] Italian seasoning – 1 tablespoon
- [ ] Marjoram – 6 sprigs
- [ ] Pepper, ground – 2 tablespoons
- [ ] Spirulina – 1 tablespoon

Garnish - Fats
- [ ] Olive oil, first cold pressing – ½ cup, plus 2 teaspoons
- [ ] Sesame oil, toasted – 2 tablespoons

Continue Feasting

Once you pass through the learning stage of raw food preparation and began to incorporate these techniques, you will be at ease with the equipment and comfortable in the art of raw cuisine. I use the techniques taught in the Raw Food Feast, but sometimes not all at once. There are times that I need fast methods and simple techniques to save time and still absorb adequate nutrition. The following recipes are included for those who need more simplicity and/or desire to abstain from food for a period of time and then return to food in a safe tangible way. These are very helpful to introduce food to the digestive tract after water fasting and juice feasting. Because they are pure and gentle on the digestive track they also make excellent baby food, nutrition for the elderly and those suffering from a digestive disorder.

Be aware that after a period of restraining from food, the temptation to overeat is extremely powerful. It is very important not to go off a fast the wrong way. Focus on freedom that leads to life, instead of succumbing in a weak moment to past indulgences that you only thought were satisfying your hunger or emotion. Some of the most common situations, such as in the grocery store or traveling to and from transporting my children to their activities, were a stumbling block. I learned that I could still maintain an active lifestyle while still managing to eat healthfully. I soon had to forgo shopping at the local conventional markets and shop health food stores to help conquer my cravings. I learned to center my attention on one isle — the fresh organic produce isle — while shopping at the

market. This may mean taking a longer route, in order to bypass particular areas of town, favorite convenient stores and fast food or fine dining restaurant. This was a very important and successful step to overcoming these temptations.

Although, I chose the fast approach of detoxing quickly through fasting, I did not quit cold turkey without first implementing healthy replacements for my vices. I searched for other satisfying options that were uplifting to my day, rather than destructive choices that caused a roller coaster of ups and downs. Some of these included substituting my favorite soda pop with a raw probiotic drink called Kombucha or my daily candy bar with a healthier treat from my local health food store. I am conscience now to never let anything become too routine, so I do not become addicted or attached to one thing. I have found that with the change of seasons and the many provisions that God has blessed us with that the choices are endless. I replace the good with the good and have so much fun when the seasons change to explore the selection.

The following is my basic blended food routine, which consists in the majority of my food consumption on a regular basis. I change the routine by incorporating the different vegetables and fruits available throughout the season. My blended foods incorporate a green smoothie and a blended soup. I have discovered that when I alternate sweet and salty this helps me remain steadfast. Also, soup leftovers can be dehydrated to make tortillas or tostadas that are topped with fresh ingredients.

Chef Mandy's Daily Raw Routine

Breakfast - Basic Green Juice
When I extract green juice, I always reserve some as a base for a green smoothie later in the morning or for lunch.

Basic Green Juice
Chard, green, 1 head
Romaine lettuce, 1 head
Celery, 1 bunch
Cucumbers, 2 medium
Apple, green, 1 medium (optional)
Choice of YL essential oil

Extract produce through a twin gear or champion juice extractor. Strain the juice for a smoother consistency, if desired. Add favorite oils, stir and enjoy.
Optional - Reserve some to make a green smoothie.

Snack - Basic Green Smoothie
When I do not have time to extract green juice, I make green smoothies for breakfast. Otherwise, I will schedule this smoothie for a refreshing snack, quick lunch or mid-afternoon snack. The optional technique of making candy from leftover smoothies is only eaten after solid food has been reintroduced through blended foods.

Fresh citrus juice and/or young coconut water, 2 cups
Reserved green juice or fresh greens such as kale, chard, cucumbers, celery, etc., 2 cups
Bananas, 2 frozen
Frozen fruit such as pineapple and/or berries, 1 cup, chopped
YL Power Meal, 1 scoop
Choice of YL essential oil

Blend all of the ingredients in a high-speed blender and enjoy.
Optional - Reserve 1 cup in the blender to make candy. Add more frozen fruit and blend until smooth. Spoon 9 tablespoons of the candy mixture onto each of 4 solid dehydrator sheets. Dehydrate at 105° F until disks peel. This will occur from approximately 12 to 24 hours. Form the candy into creative shapes.

Lunch and Dinner - Blended Soups and Wraps
These soups are as easy to prepare as smoothies and can satisfy the savory salty cravings. There is no extensive preproduction for these recipes; it requires chopping, blending and serving.

Soup Elements
There are basic elements to create simple vegetable soups. Taste buds are extremely sensitive following a water fast or juice feast. Every flavor is heightened and the simplicity of blended fruits and vegetables is appreciated more in this clean state than when the body is toxic and does not crave simple good foods. I have not included

onion or garlic as these are extremely pungent and cause the body to omit strong food odors following a fast. All pungent savory herbs, unless in the form of YL essential oils, should not be added to the diet immediately. In addition fatty oils, nuts and seeds should not be added immediately to allow for a slower transition. This is a starting point and each category can expand to include more options as you begin to recognize the other natural flavors of God's bountiful harvest.

These blended soups are an excellent way to transition and are highly recommended to restart the body's digestive organs. In addition wraps and tostadas can be made from leftover soup as the first introduction of a solid food.

Use this formula for flavor balancing and to assist the creative process.:
Base - Choice of vegetables (root, leafy and other)
Cream - Choice of creamy vegetable (avocado, coconut meat and/or zucchini)
Sweet - Choice of fruit (pear or apple)
Savory - Choice of an all-purpose seasoning (vegetable base) and other minimal spices
Salty - Choice of salty flavor (Himalayan sea salt or Nama Shoyu/ wheat-free Tamari)
Sour - Choice of acid (citrus, tomato or raw apple cider vinegar)
Liquid - Choice of liquid (filtered alkaline water, fresh extracted juice or coconut water)
Essential oils - Choice of YL essential oil (This is an optional ingredient. Have fun experimenting with the many culinary flavors.)

NOTE: For the following soups, blend all of the soup's ingredients in a high-speed blender until smooth (approximately 20 seconds). Do not over blend or the soup aerates and becomes frothy.

Tomato Tarragon Soup
Grape tomatoes, 1 pint
Red bell pepper, 1 baby, chopped
Zucchini, 1 medium, peeled and chopped
Celery, 1 medium stalk, chopped
Fuji apple, 1 medium, chopped with peel
Young coconut meat, ½ packed cup
Vegan vegetable bouillon, such as Rapunzel, 1 cube
Himalayan salt, ½ teaspoon
Filtered alkaline water, 2 cups warm to hot
YL tarragon essential oil, 1 drop

Carrot Clove Soup
Carrots, 6 medium, peeled and chopped
Zucchini, 1 medium, peeled and chopped
Pear, 1 small, chopped with peel
Young coconut meat, ½ packed cup
Fresh lemon juice, 1 teaspoon
Vegan vegetable bouillon, such as Rapunzel, 1 cube
Cumin, 1 teaspoon ground
Himalayan salt, ½ teaspoon

Filtered alkaline water, 2 cups warm to hot
YL clove essential oil, 1 drop

Butternut Cinnamon Soup
Butternut squash, 3 cups chopped
Zucchini, 1 medium, peeled and chopped
Celery, 1 medium stalk, chopped
Green apple, 1 small, chopped with peel
Red bell pepper, 1 baby, chopped
Grape tomatoes, 6
Filtered alkaline water, 2 cups warm to hot
Vegan vegetable bouillon, such as Rapunzel, 1 cube
Himalayan salt, ½ teaspoon
YL cinnamon essential oil, 1 drop

Cauliflower Black Pepper Soup
Cauliflower, 1 small head (about 3 chopped cups)
Zucchini, 1 medium, peeled and chopped
Yellow or orange bell pepper, 1 medium, chopped
Fuji apple, 1 small with peel
Nutritional yeast, 1 tablespoon
Fresh lemon juice, 1 teaspoon
Vegan vegetable bouillon, such as Rapunzel, 1 cube
Himalayan salt, ½ teaspoon
Filtered alkaline water, 2 cups warm to hot
YL black pepper essential oil, 1 drop

Corn Lemon Soup
Yellow corn kernels, 3 cups (approximately 5 corn stalks)
Zucchini, 1 medium, peeled and chopped
Celery, 1 medium stalk, chopped
Grape tomatoes, 6
Yellow bell pepper, 1 baby, chopped
Nutritional yeast, 2 tablespoons
Vegan vegetable bouillon, such as Rapunzel, 1 cube
Himalayan salt, ½ teaspoon
Filtered alkaline water, 2 cups warm to hot
YL lemon essential oil, 1 drop

Asparagus Sage Soup
Asparagus, 1pound, chopped
Young coconut meat, 1 cup packed
Celery, 1 medium stalk, chopped
Pear, 1 medium, chopped with peel
Cucumber, ½ medium, chopped

Vegan vegetable bouillon, such as Rapunzel, 1 cube
Raw apple cider vinegar, 1 teaspoon
Himalayan salt, ½ teaspoon
Filtered alkaline water, 2 cups warm to hot
YL sage essential oil, 1 drop

Broccoli Orange Soup
Broccoli florets, 3 cups, chopped
Zucchini, 1 medium, peeled and chopped
Grape tomatoes, 6
Fuji apple, 1 small, chopped with peel
Avocado, 1 medium, chopped
Nutritional yeast, 1 tablespoon
Vegan vegetable bouillon, such as Rapunzel, 1 cube
Nama Shoyu, wheat-free Tamari or raw coconut aminos, 2 tablespoons
Filtered alkaline water, 2 cups warm to hot
YL orange essential oil, 2 drops

Beet Fennel Cabbage Soup
Beets, 2 cups, chopped
Cabbage, 2 cups, chopped
Red bell pepper, 1 medium, chopped
Grape tomatoes, 14
Avocado, 1 medium, chopped
Raw apple cider vinegar, 1 teaspoon
Vegan vegetable bouillon, such as Rapunzel, 1 cube
Himalayan salt, ½ teaspoon
Filtered alkaline water, 2 cups warm to hot
YL fennel essential oil, 1 drop

Vegetable Dill Soup
Carrots, 2 medium, peeled
Celery, 1 medium stalk, chopped
Red bell pepper, 1 baby, chopped
Cucumber, ½ medium, chopped with peel
Grape tomatoes, 12
Lacinato kale, 1 leaf, chopped
Green chard, 1 leaf, chopped
Spinach, 1 handful (approximately ½ packed cup)
Fuji apple, 1 small, chopped with peel
Avocado, 1 medium, chopped
Vegan vegetable bouillon, such as Rapunzel, 1 cube
Himalayan salt, ½ teaspoon
Filtered alkaline water, 2 cups warm to hot
YL dill essential oil, 1 drop

Wraps and Tortillas

Optional - Reserve 2 cups of soup in the blender to make wraps and tortillas. Add ⅓ cup flax meal and blend until smooth. Pour two disks onto each of 2 solid dehydrator sheets. Flatten with an offset spatula to ¼ inch thick. Dehydrate at 105°F for 4 hours or until ready to peel. Flip onto mesh-lined dehydrator trays. For wraps dry for an additional 2 hours, careful to keep flexible. For tortillas dry until crispy. Fill or top with mashed avocado to replace mayonnaise, sliced tomatoes, baby greens and/or sprouts and sprinkle with an all-purpose seasoning, if desired.

Dessert

For the occasional dessert or snack, I am satisfied with fresh or dried fruit with soaked and dehydrated nuts. I do not eat these immediately following a water fast or juice feast until blended foods have been added for a period of time.

Final Encouragement

As I rotate through these structured plans, I discover that my being has the will to conform to physical, emotional and spiritual renewal. Through this form of sacrifice, I desire to pray. When I find that I am on a path of self-indulgence, my focus returns to me. I prefer living a fasted life in order to engage in spiritual warfare. Jesus spoke about times when fasting from food was the key to removing principalities and spiritual forces in a realm that we cannot see. These forces are very destructive and at times must be expelled through a focused and selfless fasted life.

Deliverance is evident as one enters into a water fast and rapid detox takes place. During detox the focus is upon physical health. Once energy is restored, prayer is feasible. When I sacrifice food I am present, conscience and focused to concentrate on the task at hand. I challenge everyone to experience this kind of freedom by rotating through the raw food feast, juice feast, water fast and then return safely with juicing and blended foods. I have journaled my experiences during these raw times and enjoy anticipating the move of the spirit in myself and in the lives of others. I hope you will too.

Raw Resources

Raw and living products are manufactured ingredients that can be purchased and used for many recipes and as compliments to dishes. Most are easily accessible through a local health food store or on the Internet. There are many companies who supply the same product, so it is crucial to research various companies and their products before purchasing. It is best to use high-quality products from conscientious manufactures who have the best intentions for the consumer and the environment. Below is the list of products and Chef Mandy's preferred brands that may be purchased from any local health or specialty grocery store, with the exception of Irish Moss, which can easily be ordered from the Web site listed.

Sea Vegetables
Dulse
Dulse and Maine Coast Sea Vegetables
– www.seaveg.com

Nori
Emerald Cove (untoasted dried seaweed)
– www.great-eastern-sun.com

Irish Moss
WIF Global – www.wifglobal.com

Oils
Cacao Butter (optional for chocolate recipe)
ELF (Essential Living Foods) –
www.essentiallivingfoods.com

Virgin Coconut Oil
Tropical Traditions Gold Label Standard –
www.tropicaltraditions.com
Cocopura –http://vivapura.net/index.
php?main_page=index&cPath=65

Olive Oil
Living Tree Community –
www.livingtreecommunity.com

Sesame Oil
Napa Valley Naturals – www.worldpantry.
com

White Truffle Oil
da Rosario (organic truffle-flavored olive oil) – multiple sources

Spices/Seasonings
Salty
Himalayan Sea Salt
Sustainable Sourcing, LLC –
www.himalasalt.com
ELF (Essential Living Foods) –
www.essentiallivingfoods.com

Savory
Five-Spice Powder
Frontier – www.frontiercoop.com

Cumin
Frontier – www.frontiercoop.com or
Simply Organic – www.
simplyorganicfoods.com

Italian Seasonings
Simply Organic – www.
simplyorganicfoods.com

Onion Powder
Frontier – www.frontiercoop.com or
Simply Organic – www.
simplyorganicfoods.com

Turmeric Powder
Frontier – www.frontiercoop.com or
Simply Organic – www.
simplyorganicfoods.com

White Peppercorns
Frontier – www.frontiercoop.com

Spicy
Anise
Frontier – www.frontiercoop.com

Mustard Seed, Yellow
Frontier – www.frontiercoop.com or
Simply Organic –
www.simplyorganicfoods.com

Onion White Flakes
Frontier – www.frontiercoop.com or
Simply Organic –
www.simplyorganicfoods.com

Sweet
Cinnamon Powder
Frontier – www.frontiercoop.com or
Simply Organic –
www.simplyorganicfoods.com

Nutmeg Powder
Frontier – www.frontiercoop.com or
Simply Organic –
www.simplyorganicfoods.com

Paprika
Frontier – www.frontiercoop.com or
Simply Organic –
www.simplyorganicfoods.com

Vanilla Powder
ELF (Essential Living Foods) –
www.essentiallivingfoods.com

Flavorings[1]
Vanilla (flavor alcohol-free)
Frontier – www.frontiercoop.com

Almond (flavor alcohol-free)
Frontier – www.frontiercoop.com

Condiments
Apple cider vinegar
Bragg – www.bragg.com
or

Raw Coconut Vinegar
Coconut Secret –
www.coconutsecret.com

Capers
Mediterranean Organic –
www.mediterraneanorganic.com

Chickpea Miso
South River or Miso Master Organic –
www.great-eastern-sun.com

Multidophilus Powder
Solaray – www.solaray.com

Nama Shoyu
Ohsawa –
www.goldminenaturalfood.com
or
Wheat-free Tamari
San-J – www.san-j.com
or
Raw Coconut Aminos
Coconut Secret –
www.coconutsecret.com

Red Curry Paste
Thai Kitchen – www.thaikitchen.com

Sundried Tomatoes
Mediterranean Organic –
www.mediterraneanorganic.com

Superfoods
Cacao Powder
Navitas Naturals –
www.navitasnaturals.com
ELF (Essential Living Foods) –
www.essentiallivingfoods.com
or
Carob Powder (roasted)
Frontier – www.frontiercoop.com

Dried herbs
Mountain Rose Herbs –
www.mountainroseherbs.com

---

1   Instead of imitation or alcohol-filled extracts, choose
alcohol-free flavorings.

Kitchen Equipment
Food Dehydrators
To purchase an Excalibur dehydrator, go to www.chefmandy.com.

High-Speed Blenders
To purchase a Vita-Mix, go to www.chefmandy.com.

Juice Extractors
For a list of recommended juicers, go to www.chefmandy.com.

Food processors
Cuisinart – www.cuisinart.com

Spiralizers
To purchase a spiralizer, go to www.chefmandy.com.

Water Systems
For alkaline/ionized water systems, go to www.chefmandy.com.

Essential Oils
To purchase Young Living essential oils and cleansing products, go to www.youngliving.com or call 1-800-371-2928. You must have an Enroller and/or Sponsor number. This is the person who shared this book with you or who first introduced you to Young Living Essential Oils.

Index

Notes